Mastering Drupal 8 Views

Accelerate your development process using Drupal 8
Views with this advanced, practical guide

Gregg Marshall

BIRMINGHAM - MUMBAI

Mastering Drupal 8 Views

First published: May 2016

Production reference: 1180516

Published by Packt Publishing Ltd.
Livery Place
35 Livery Street
Birmingham B3 2PB, UK.

ISBN 978-1-78588-696-6

www.packtpub.com

Credits

Author
Gregg Marshall

Reviewer
Adrian Ababei

Commissioning Editor
Amarabha Banerjee

Acquisition Editor
Reshma Raman

Content Development Editor
Sachin Karnani

Technical Editor
Taabish Khan

Copy Editors
Shruti Iyer
Sonia Mathur

Project Coordinator
Nikhil Nair

Proofreader
Safis Editing

Indexer
Rekha Nair

Graphics
Jason Monterio

Production Coordinator
Manu Joseph

Cover Work
Manu Joseph

Foreword

Without Views, Drupal wouldn't be Drupal. It wouldn't be powering more than 1 million websites*—5% of all websites that have an identifiable CMS**—and there wouldn't be more than 35,000 developer accounts on Drupal.org***.

There are three keys to building dynamic, content-first websites. The first is the ability to model semantic data structures (Content Construction Kit used to be a contributed module; now, it has become entities and fields in Drupal core). The second is selecting what content you want based on any given criteria (part of Views is a database query-building UI). And finally, displaying it how and where you want (the other part of Views is a set of configurable display options ranging from HTML lists and tables to RSS feeds to web service endpoints and more).

Does this sound complicated? Views can be daunting for the first-time user. But in the hands of an experienced Drupal expert, the power and flexibility of Views brings some of the world's most important and interesting websites to life. Another consequence of its complexity is how difficult it has been for me to explain its use to others, even to figure out where to start.

After reading this unusual technical book, it is clear to me that Gregg Marshall has lived and breathed Drupal and Views for many years. This is not just another dull technical manual full of lists of dry facts. Gregg has lived up to the challenge of explaining Views, and not only does he do that, but he also shares his knowledge and experience in an engaging way. He's tied together a collection of useful exercises with the fictitious story of a Drupal service provider, a Drupal client, and her cat.

> *That evening Lynn logged into the new site. Clicking on the* **Manage** *menu item, she clicked on the* **Structure** *submenu item, and at the bottom of the list displayed on the* **Structure** *page, she clicked on the* **Views** *option.*

> *About that time Jackson came in and settled into his spot near her terminal. "Hi Jackson, ready to explore Views with me?"*

Looking at the Views administration page, Lynn noticed there were already a number of Views defined. Scanning the list, she said "Look, Jackson, Drupal 8 uses Views for administration pages. This means we can customize them to fit our way of doing things. I like Drupal 8 already." Jackson purred. Lynn studied the Views administration page.

The exercises cover the myriad facets of the Views interface and options and contain tips that clearly come from Gregg's practical experiences in using this tool. The story elements worked well as a vehicle to keep me engaged with the exercises. They also help link situations familiar to Drupal service providers and clients to the practical use of Views to solve them.

Views has been one of Drupal's killer apps since its introduction; it was the most installed contributed module—at 900,000 reported installs****—before it was merged into the core. Drupal 8 was released in November 2015 with a slew of new features, refinements, and lots of tricks up its sleeve. These tricks in Drupal's core include comprehensive multilingual capabilities, improved accessibility, user interfaces to build RESTful APIs and web services, structured semantic data throughout, mobile-first architecture, and plenty more, including Views built right into the Drupal core!

Thank you, Gregg!

Jeffrey A. "jam" McGuire
Evangelist, Developer Relations, Acquia

*https://www.drupal.org/project/usage/drupal

**http://w3techs.com/technologies/details/cm-drupal/all/all

***https://en.wikipedia.org/wiki/Drupal#Community

****https://medium.com/@tacopotze/some-facts-on-the-top-5-000-drupal-modules-e4d685adc081#.r5x6mutd0

About the Author

Gregg Marshall has been using Drupal since 2006. While he installed Drupal 5, his first production site was Drupal 6. He started his career as a software engineer, switched to sales/marketing in an unrelated industry, and drifted back to development. After attending DrupalCon 2010 in San Francisco, Gregg switched from channel marketing that used Drupal for microsites to being a full-time Drupal developer.

Gregg works as a consultant/contractor, frequently mentoring in-house development teams on Drupal best practices. His current contract is with WebNY, where he serves as the senior Drupal architect for the state of New York, helping build a single platform for all the state's websites.

Gregg is a speaker at Drupal Camps and is a professional speaker to 30+ associations and corporate meetings. He has over 400 published articles in a variety of publications. Gregg has a bachelor's degree in chemistry, a master's degree in electrical engineering, and a master's degree in business administration. He is an Acquia Certified Drupal Grand Master.

Acknowledgements

To my wife, Lorraine, who has been completely supportive of writing this book while also commuting to New York to work, and my children, Christopher, Patrick, and Amanda, who have stepped in to free up my time.

I would like to thank the team at WebNY, who have been great to work with as my two month contract enters its fourth year. I would like to acknowledge especially Jennifer Warner, Meredith Case, and Jim Kavanaugh, who encouraged me in this endeavor.

A special thank you to the technical reviewer, Adrian Ababei, who has offered a ton of great suggestions and pointed me to a number of Views options I hadn't noticed before.

Finally, a thank you to Dries Buytaert for Drupal and Earl Miles for Views; obviously, without them, this book would be empty.

About the Reviewer

Adrian Ababei is a senior Drupal developer and architect with over 14 years of experience in designing, architecting, implementing, and supporting interactive websites, applications, and solutions. He has more than 11 years of experience in working with Drupal alone.

During the last 5 years, he was the lead Drupal developer and technical director for a Toronto-based Drupal shop, AllWeb247.

> I would love to be part of another Packt project and review another Drupal book. I would like to thank my family for their support and love: George, Alina, mom, dad, and Camy.

www.PacktPub.com

eBooks, discount offers, and more

Did you know that Packt offers eBook versions of every book published, with PDF and ePub files available? You can upgrade to the eBook version at www.PacktPub.com and as a print book customer, you are entitled to a discount on the eBook copy. Get in touch with us at customercare@packtpub.com for more details.

At www.PacktPub.com, you can also read a collection of free technical articles, sign up for a range of free newsletters and receive exclusive discounts and offers on Packt books and eBooks.

https://www2.packtpub.com/books/subscription/packtlib

Do you need instant solutions to your IT questions? PacktLib is Packt's online digital book library. Here, you can search, access, and read Packt's entire library of books.

Why subscribe?

- Fully searchable across every book published by Packt
- Copy and paste, print, and bookmark content
- On demand and accessible via a web browser

Table of Contents

Preface

To make this book a little easier to read, I use a story of a Drupal user who has advanced to the point of being able to do their own site building. Setting the stage for the story woven into the book, let's start with a bit of background for the story.

Blue Drop Realty started business in 2002 as a part-time "hobby" of the owner, Lynn. As their business grew, they decided to build a website in 2005 using Dreamweaver to lay out their pages. This worked okay for about 5 years, but it was taking too much of Lynn's time to update the pages, and the site's design was starting to look dated. The business had grown enough that they had a new website developed by Fancy Websites, Inc., who used Drupal 6 to build the new website. With Drupal, the office manager and even some of the salespeople were able to make changes to the pages.

Lynn is joined in this story by her grey tabby cat, Jackson, an alley cat, literally, who adopted Lynn's family a couple of years ago. Once Jackson got comfortable with the new surroundings and being around a family, he frequently would curl up on Lynn's desk next to her monitor when she would work at night. Lynn has gotten into the habit of talking to Jackson as she works—he has proven to be a good listener.

Their Drupal 6 website is still working fine for Blue Drop Realty, but knowing that when Drupal 8 is released, support for Drupal 6 will end shortly afterward, Lynn is considering options to upgrade to the latest version of Drupal. She has gotten comfortable with Drupal 6 and even makes some "programming" changes to the site using the Drupal user interface as a site administrator. Lynn was able to add a news release content type herself, but she had to have Fancy Websites, Inc. create the views to display a list of releases on a news page. As she worked with Drupal, Lynn learned how to modify some views and even build a relatively simple list view on her own.

Jim is the developer at Fancy Websites, Inc., which built Lynn's original Drupal 6 site. As Lynn learns and becomes more comfortable with Drupal, Jim will morph from the developer who built the site to Lynn's mentor, as she herself will grow from a new content editor to site builder. More than anything else, Jim will help Lynn whenever she gets stuck.

A short history

Drupal is an open source content management system used by over 1,200,000 websites. It started as a message board written by Dries Buytaert in 2000 while in college at University of Antwerp. The original site Dries built was drop.org, a mistake when he went to register dorp.org, dorp being Dutch for village. When he decided to open source the software in January 2000, he named it Drupal.

Views has been described as the report writer for Drupal. It is that and a whole lot more.

Drupal progressed rapidly through many revisions, with Drupal 4 released in June 2002, Drupal 5 in January 2007, Drupal 6 in February 2008, and Drupal 7 in January 2010. Drupal 8, which is a major rearchitecting of Drupal, has taken almost 5 years, a third of Drupal's total lifetime, to be completed.

In May 2006, a contributed CCK module, Content Construction Kit, was released for Drupal 4.7 and became the standard for defining fields via the user interface, replacing the older Flexinode module, which dates back to February 2004. Before this, any modifications to the basic structure of a node would require manually defining database tables for a field and creating all the functions to create, edit, display, and delete the field when the corresponding node is changed or viewed.

The Views module was first created (at least the first commit was made to it) on November 25, 2005. The first release, 4.6.x-1.x-dev, was on December 1, 2005. The first non-development release, 4.7.x-1.0, was almost a year later on November 11, 2006. The first release contained 3,177 executable lines of PHP. The current Drupal 7 release of Views contains 57,155 lines of non-comment PHP. Its supporting module, CTools, contains another 39,939 lines. The Drupal 8 version of Views contains 58,925 lines, with most of CTools absorbed into Drupal core. Just as telling is that Drupal 8 Views has 19,921 lines of tests, where Drupal 7 only has 9,238 and Drupal 4.7 has none.

Before the Views module, any display not contained in the Drupal core or a contributed module required manually creating the necessary SQL queries, executing them against MySQL (at the time the only database supported by Drupal), and then taking the results and formatting them into HTML. This required significant PHP and MySQL programming experience. With the release of Views, users with limited programming experience could create powerful displays from the user interface.

At the time of writing, Views for Drupal 7 has almost 600 supporting contributed modules. As of the release of Drupal 8, Views for Drupal 8 has 65 supporting contributed modules, but many module contributors are just starting to port modules to Drupal 8, so the number will rise dramatically in the months to come.

Drupal is always changing

This book was started just as Drupal 8.0.0 was about to be released and was finished shortly before Drupal 8.1.0 was about to be released. In between were 8.0.1 through 8.0.5, a new release about every two weeks. With each release, a number of issues were resolved. Some of those issues affect how Views operates or the wording of some screen text or prompts. The evolution of Drupal and Views will continue long after this book is done. As a result, it is very likely that some screens and prompts described here might not match your copy of Drupal exactly. The differences are minor changes in wording to improve the understandability or clarify the meaning. Do not be alarmed if there are small differences between this book and Views when you use it. These differences will be mostly cosmetic, although it is possible that a new option might appear.

What this book covers

The first thing you will notice is that this isn't your traditional technical book written in a dry third-party tone. It reads a bit more like a novel, following Lynn as she learns how to master Views. Jackson, her cat, and Jim, her mentor, are along for the ride and to let the story change viewpoints from time to time (and to give Lynn "people" to talk to).

Views is an amazing part of Drupal 8. I hope you will enjoy this approach to explaining it.

Chapter 1, Up and Running with Views, deals with the Views main administration page and setting pages and does a quick run-through of View's edit screen by modifying an existing core view.

Chapter 2, Views from Scratch, starts the in-depth exploration of Views, starting with building a simple property listing that most real estate sites might have. We will define some Views terms such as View Types, displays, Display Formats, and Display Contents. We'll end with an interesting view that displays selected events from Drupal's watchdog log to users that might normally not be able to see them.

Chapter 3, Sorting and Filtering, introduces sorting and filtering. Sorting lets you specify the order you want your results to be displayed in. We will move on to limiting which results are even displayed using filtering. You can also expose a filter to the user and let them select which results to show. Finally, we'll show how to group the results when a view results in multiple rows for each value.

Chapter 4, Contextual Filters, takes filtering to the next level by adding contextual filters. Contextual filters use the URL to pass the selection criteria to the filter.

Chapter 5, Relationships, shows how to use relationships to gain access to even more data to display. Using the built-in entity reference, any reference field can be used to add all the fields in the referenced content to the available fields list.

Chapter 6, Add-on Modules, adds more Display Formats using add-on contributed modules. Using add-on modules, we can add a slideshow or a rotating carousel as easily as enabling the module, installing the JavaScript library it uses, and defining a very simple view.

Chapter 7, Field Rewrites, is about field rewrites. It is uncommon that the default output of a view exactly meets your needs, including the if-then-else values, in which if a condition is true, one value is displayed, but if it isn't true, another value is displayed.

Chapter 8, Customizing Views, covers the rest of the options in the center column of the view edit page, such as custom headers, footers, and special messages if a set of filters (defined, exposed, or contextual) results in no results.

Chapter 9, Advanced View Settings, deals with all of the advanced settings except contextual filters and relationships, which are covered in earlier chapters.

Chapter 10, Theming Views, winds up the book with how to theme or style the output of Views. Some CSS support can be easily added through the user interface; other, more complex changes might require replacing the Twig templates used by Views with custom templates that do manipulations not possible from the user interface.

What you need for this book

Throughout the book, we have used Google Chrome as our browser. You can use any modern web browser and text editor, but I highly recommend you use this open source software to make any of the projects discussed in this book.

To follow along and try these Views, you will need a functioning installation of Drupal 8. Acquia Dev Desktop is an easy way to install Drupal on Windows or Mac (https://www.acquia.com/downloads). Alternatively, you can use WAMP or MAMP to install Drupal 8 locally. Or, you can also use free hosting at Acquia Cloud (https://www.acquia.com/free) or Pantheon (https://pantheon.io/).

For quick experimenting, `https://simplytest.me/` offers free sites that can be created in a few minutes and last up to 24 hours. For other environments, take a look at the Drupal 8 requirements at `https://www.drupal.org/requirements`.

Who this book is for

This book is for web developers, web designers, and website administrators who use Drupal 8, have some basic knowledge of managing and developing apps with Drupal, and want to get an advanced, practical knowledge of Views and how to leverage them in Drupal 8 applications.

Given that Drupal 8's version of Views is a port of the Drupal 7 version (Views 7.x-3.x), much, if not most, of the book is just as applicable to Drupal 7. The user interface is virtually identical, but some options have more choices.

Conventions

In this book, you will find a number of text styles that distinguish between different kinds of information. Here are some examples of these styles and an explanation of their meaning.

Code words in text, database table names, folder names, filenames, file extensions, pathnames, dummy URLs, user input, and Twitter handles are shown as follows: "Each row is wrapped in `<LI>` tags."

A block of code is set as follows:

```
SELECT node_field_data.title AS node_field_data_title, node_field_
data.nid AS nid
FROM
{node_field_data} node_field_data
WHERE (( (node_field_data.status = '1') AND (node_field_data.type IN
('open_house')) ))
ORDER BY node_field_data_title DESC
LIMIT 10 OFFSET 0
```

New terms and **important words** are shown in bold. Words that you see on the screen, for example, in menus or dialog boxes, appear in the text like this: "She clicked on the **Apply (all displays)** button."

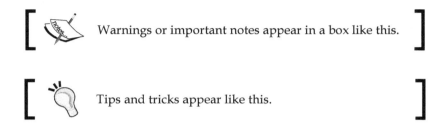

Warnings or important notes appear in a box like this.

Tips and tricks appear like this.

Reader feedback

Feedback from our readers is always welcome. Let us know what you think about this book—what you liked or disliked. Reader feedback is important for us as it helps us develop titles that you will really get the most out of.

To send us general feedback, simply e-mail feedback@packtpub.com, and mention the book's title in the subject of your message.

If there is a topic that you have expertise in and you are interested in either writing or contributing to a book, see our author guide at www.packtpub.com/authors.

Customer support

Now that you are the proud owner of a Packt book, we have a number of things to help you to get the most from your purchase.

Downloading the color images of this book

We also provide you with a PDF file that has color images of the screenshots/diagrams used in this book. The color images will help you better understand the changes in the output. You can download this file from https://www.packtpub.com/sites/default/files/downloads/MasteringDrupal8Views_ColorImages.pdf.

Errata

Although we have taken every care to ensure the accuracy of our content, mistakes do happen. If you find a mistake in one of our books—maybe a mistake in the text or the code—we would be grateful if you could report this to us. By doing so, you can save other readers from frustration and help us improve subsequent versions of this book. If you find any errata, please report them by visiting http://www.packtpub.com/submit-errata, selecting your book, clicking on the **Errata Submission Form** link, and entering the details of your errata. Once your errata are verified, your submission will be accepted and the errata will be uploaded to our website or added to any list of existing errata under the Errata section of that title.

To view the previously submitted errata, go to https://www.packtpub.com/books/content/support and enter the name of the book in the search field. The required information will appear under the **Errata** section.

Piracy

Piracy of copyrighted material on the Internet is an ongoing problem across all media. At Packt, we take the protection of our copyright and licenses very seriously. If you come across any illegal copies of our works in any form on the Internet, please provide us with the location address or website name immediately so that we can pursue a remedy.

Please contact us at copyright@packtpub.com with a link to the suspected pirated material.

We appreciate your help in protecting our authors and our ability to bring you valuable content.

Questions

If you have a problem with any aspect of this book, you can contact us at questions@packtpub.com, and we will do our best to address the problem.

Up and Running with Views

1

Drupal 8 was released on November 19, 2015, after almost 5 years of development by more than 3,000 members of the Drupal community. Drupal 8 is the largest refactoring in the project's history.

One of the most important changes in Drupal 8 was the inclusion of the most popular contributed module, **Views**. Similar to including CCK in Drupal 7, adding Views to Drupal 8 influenced how Drupal operates, as many of the administration pages, such as the content list page, are now views that can be modified or extended by site builders.

Every site builder needs to master the Views module to really take advantage of Drupal's content structuring capabilities by giving site builders the ability to create lists of content formatted in many different ways. A single piece of content can be used for different displays, and all the content in each view is dynamically created when a visitor comes to a page. It is so important, it was the only contributed module included in the Acquia Site Builder certification examination for Drupal 7.

In this chapter, we will discuss the following topics:

- Looking at the Views administration page
- Reviewing the general Views module settings
- Modifying one of the views from Drupal core to create a specialized administrative page

Drupal is always changing

This book was started just after Drupal 8.0.0 was released and has been finished shortly before Drupal 8.1.0 is about to be released. In between are 8.0.1 through 8.0.5, a new release about every two weeks. With each release, a number of issues are resolved. Some of those issues affect how Views operate or the wording of some screen text or prompts. The evolution of Drupal and Views will continue long after this book is done. As a result, it is very likely that some screens and prompts described here might not match your copy of Drupal exactly. The differences are minor changes in wording to improve the understandability or clarify the meaning. *Do not be alarmed if there are small differences between this book and Views when you use it.* These differences will be mostly cosmetic, although it is possible a new option might appear.

Drupal 8 is here, should I upgrade?

"Jim, this is Lynn, how are things at Fancy Websites?"

"Hi Lynn, things are going well."

Lynn continued, "I read that Drupal 8 is being released on November 19. From our conversations this year, I guess that means it is time to upgrade our current Drupal 6 site. Should I upgrade to Drupal 7 or Drupal 8?"

"Lynn, we're really excited that Drupal 8 is finally ready. It is a game changer, and I can name 10 reasons why Drupal 8 is the way to go":

- Mobile device compatibility is built into Drupal 8's DNA. Analytics show that 32% of your site traffic is coming from buyers using phones, and that's up from only 19% compared to last year.

- Multilingual is baked in and really works, so we can go ahead and add the Spanish version of the site we have been talking about.

- There's a new theme engine called Twig that will make styling the new site much easier. It's time to update the look of your site; it's looking pretty outdated compared to the competition.

- Web services are built in. When you're ready to add an app for your customer's phones, Drupal 8 will be ready.

- There are lots of new field types built in for useful stuff such as telephone numbers, e-mail addresses, and more, so we won't need to add half a dozen contributed modules to let you build your content types.

- Drupal 8 is built using industry standards. This was a huge change you won't see, but it means that our shop will be able to recruit new developers more easily.

- The configuration is now stored in code. Finally, we'll have a way for you to develop on your local computer and move your changes to staging and then to production without having to rebuild content types and views manually over and over.

- The WYSIWYG editor is built in. The complex setup we went through to get the right buttons and make the output work won't be necessary in Drupal 8.

- There's a nice tour capability built in so that you can set up custom "how to" demonstrations for your new users. This should free up a lot of your time, which is good given how you are growing.

- I've saved the best for last. Your favorite module, Views, is now built into core! Between Fields in Drupal 7 and now Views in Drupal 8, you've got the tools to extend your site built right into core.

"The bottom line is I can't imagine not going ahead and upgrading to Drupal 8. Views in core is reason enough. Why don't I set up a Drupal 8 installation on your development server so that you can start playing with Drupal 8? We're not doing any development work on your site right now, and we still have staging to test any updates."

"That sounds great, Jim! Let me know when I can log in."

Less than an hour later, the e-mail arrived; the Drupal 8 development site was set up and ready for Lynn to start experimenting.

Based on the existing Drupal 6 site, Lynn set up four content types with the same fields she had on the current site. These content types are outlined in *Appendix, Content Types for a Sample Site*. Jim was able to use the built-in migrate module to move some of her data to the new site.

Lynn was ready to start exploring Views in Drupal 8.

Looking at the Views administration page

That evening, Lynn logged into the new site. Clicking on the **Manage** menu item, she then clicked on the **Structure** submenu item, and at the bottom of the list displayed on the **Structure** page, she clicked on the **Views** option.

About that time, Jackson came in and settled into his spot near her terminal. "Hi Jackson, ready to explore Views with me?"

Looking at the Views administration page, Lynn noticed there were already a number of Views defined. Scanning the list, she said "Look Jackson, Drupal 8 uses Views for administration pages. This means we can customize them to fit our way of doing things. I like Drupal 8 already!". Jackson purred. Lynn studied the Views administration page shown here:

Views administration page

As Lynn looked at each view, the listing looked familiar; she had seen the same kind of listing on her Drupal 6 site. Trying the **OPERATIONS** pull-down menu on the first view, she saw that the options were **Edit**, **Duplicate**, **Disable**, and **Delete**. "That's pretty clear; I guess Duplicate is the same as Clone on my old version of Views. I can change a view, create a new one using this one as a template, make it temporarily unavailable, or wipe it completely off the face of the earth."

"I wonder what kind of settings there are on the **Settings** tab of this listing page. Look, Jackson, there's a couple of subtabs hiding on the **Settings** page." As Lynn didn't want to mess up her new Drupal site, she called Jim. "Hi, Jim. Can you give me a quick rundown on the Views **Settings** tab?"

"Sure," he replied.

Views settings

"Looking at the Views **Settings** tab, you'll notice two subtabs, **Basic** and **Advanced**. Select the advanced settings tab by clicking on **Advanced** to show the following display:

The Views advanced settings configuration page

Views advanced settings

Let's look at the **Advanced** tab first since you'll probably never use these settings.

The first option, **Disable views data caching**, shouldn't be checked unless you are having issues with views not updating when the data changes. Even then, you should probably disable caching on a per-view basis using the caching setting in the view's edit page in the third column, labeled **Advanced**, near the bottom of the column. Disabling views' data caching can really slow down the page loads on your site.

You might actually use the **Advanced** settings tab if you need to clear all the Views' caches, which you would do by clicking on the **Clear Views' cache** button.

The other advanced setting is **DEBUGGING** with an **Add Views signature to all SQL queries** checkbox. Unless you are using MySQL's logs to debug queries, which only an advanced developer would do, you aren't going to want this overhead added to Views queries, so just leave it unselected.

Views basic settings

Moving to the **Basic** tab, there are a number of settings that might be handy, and I'd recommend changing the default settings. Click on **Basic** to show the following display:

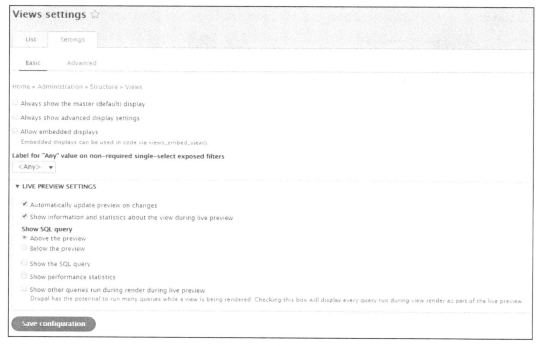

The Views basic settings configuration page

The first option, **Always show the master (default) display**, might or might not be useful. If you create a new view and don't select either create a page or create a block (or provide a REST export if this module is enabled), then a default view display is created called master. If you select either option or both, then page and/or block view displays are created; generally you won't see master. It's there; it's just hidden.

Sometimes, it is handy to be able to edit or use the master display. While I don't like creating a lot of displays in each view, sometimes I do create two or three if the content being displayed is very similar. An obvious example is when you want to display the same blog listing as either a page or in a block on other pages. The same teaser information is displayed, just in different ways. So, having the two displays in the same view makes sense.

 Just make sure when you customize each display that any changes you make are set to only apply to the current display and not all displays. Otherwise, you might make changes you hadn't planned on in the other displays. Most of the time, you will see a pull-down menu that defaults to **All displays**, but you can select **This page (override)** to have the setting change apply only to this display.

Using the master display lets you create information that will be the same in all the displays you are creating; then, you can create and customize the different displays. Using our blog example, you may create a master display that has a basic list of titles, with the titles linking to the full blog post. Then, you can create a blog display page, and using the **This page (override)** option, you can add summaries, add more links, and set the results to 10 per page. Using the master display, you can go back and add a display block that shows only the last five blog posts without any pager, again applying each setting only to the block display. You might then go back to the master display and create a second block that uses the tags to select five blog posts that are related, again making sure that the changes are applied to the current block and not all displays.

Finally, when you want to change something that will affect all the displays, make the change on the master display, and this time, use the **All displays** option to make sure the other displays are updated. In our blog example, you might decide to change the CSS class used to display the titles to apply formatting from the theme; you probably want this to look the same in every possible display of the blog posts.

 CSS and theming is covered in *Chapter 10, Theming Views*.

The next basic setting for Views is **Allow embedded displays**. You will not enable this option; it is for developers who will use Views-generated content in their custom code. However, if you see it enabled, don't disable it; doing this would likely break something on your site using this feature.

The last setting before the **LIVE PREVIEW SETTINGS** fieldset is **Label for "Any" value on non-required single-select exposed filters**, which lets you pick either <Any> or -Any- as the format for exposed filters that would allow a user to ignore the filter.

Live Preview Settings

There are several **LIVE PREVIEW SETTINGS** fieldsets I like to enable because they make debugging your views easier. If the **LIVE PREVIEW SETTINGS** fieldset is closed (if these options are not showing), click on the title next to the arrow, and it will open. It will look similar to this:

LIVE PREVIEW SETTINGS

 I generally enable the **Automatically update preview on changes** option. This way, any change I make to the view when I edit it shows the results that would occur after each change. Seeing things change right away shows me whether a change will have an effect I'm not expecting.

A lot of Views options can be tricky to understand, so a bit of trial and error is often required. Hence, expect to make a change and not see what you expect; just change the setting back, rethink the problem, and try again. Almost always, you'll get the answer eventually. If you have a view that is really complex and very slow, you can always disable the live preview while you edit the view by selecting the **Auto preview** option in the gray **Preview** bar just under all the view's settings.

The next two options control whether Views will display the SQL query generated by the Views options you selected in the edit screen.

 I like to display the SQL query, so I will select the **Above the preview** option under **Show SQL query** and then select the **Show the SQL query** checkbox that follows it.

If you don't check the **Show the SQL query** option, it doesn't matter what you select for above or below the preview, and if you expect to see the SQL queries and don't, it is likely that you set one option and not the other. Showing the SQL query can be confusing at first, but after a while, you'll find it handy to figure out what is going on, especially if you have relationships (or should have relationships and don't realize it). And, of course, if you can't read the query, you can always e-mail me for a translation to English.

The next option, **Show performance statistics**, is handy when trying to figure out why a Views-generated page is loading slowly. But usually, this isn't an issue you'd be thinking of, so I'd leave it off. You want to focus on getting the right information to display exactly the way you want without thinking about the performance. If we later decide it's too slow, the developer we'll assign to it will use this information and turn the option on in development.

The same is true about **Show other queries run during render during live preview**. This information is handy to figure out performance issues and occasionally a display formatting issue during theming, but it isn't something you as a nonprogrammer should be worried about. Seeing all the extra queries can be confusing and intimidating, yet it doesn't really offer you any help creating a view.

"Oh, don't forget to click on **Save configuration** if you change any settings. I don't know how many times I've forgotten to save a configuration change in Drupal and then wondered why my change hasn't stuck. Does this help?"

"Thanks Jim, that is great. I owe you a coffee next time we get together."

Hanging up the phone, Lynn said, "What do you think, Jackson? Let's start off by creating a property maintenance page for our salespeople to use. I think I'll get a quick win by modifying one of Drupal's core views."

Adapting an existing View

Lynn will use her knowledge from using Views on her existing Drupal site, moving quickly, but we'll come back to really dig into the view edit screen in later chapters when she's building views from scratch and improving them in successive revisions.

The existing content page provided by Views is general purpose and offers lots of options, and not all these options are appropriate for all content editors. This page looks like this:

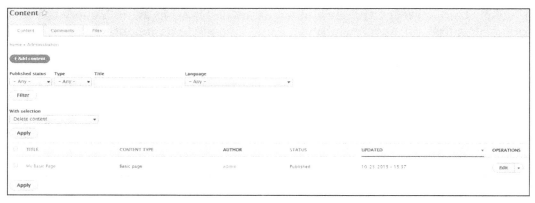

Drupal's standard content listing page

Lynn started creating her property maintenance page by going to the Views listing page (**Manage | Structure | Views**) and selecting **Duplicate** from the **OPERATIONS** pull-down menu on the right-hand side of this row. On the next screen, she named the view **Property Maintenance** and clicked on the **Duplicate** button. When the view edit screen appeared, she was ready to adapt it to her needs. First, she selected the **Page** display, assuming the **Always show the master (default) display** setting was already selected; otherwise, the **Page** display will be selected by default as it is the only display in this view.

Remember that any change made in the view edit page isn't saved until you click on the **Save** button. Also, unsaved changes won't show up when the page/block is displayed. If you make a change, look at it using another browser or tab, and if you don't see the change reflected, it is likely that you didn't save the change you just made.

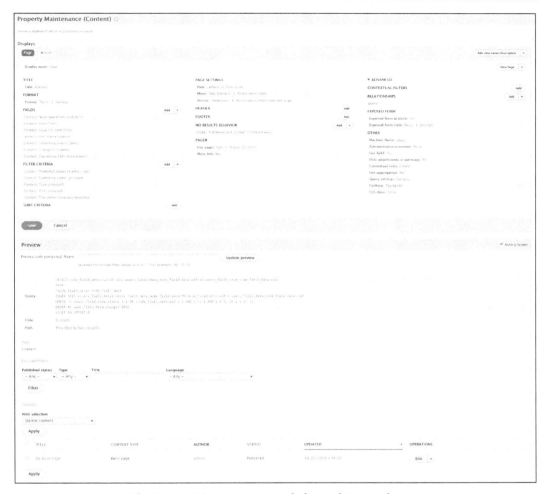

The Property Maintenance screen before making any changes

Editing the Property Maintenance view

Starting with the left-hand side column of the view edit screen, Lynn changed the title by clicking on the **Content** link next to the **Title** label. She changed the title to **Property Maintenance**. Moving down the column, Lynn decided that the table display and settings were okay on the original screen and skipped them.

Under the **FIELDS** section, Lynn decided to delete the **Content: Node operations bulk form**, **Content: Type (Content Type)**, and **(author) User: Name (Author)** fields/ columns as they weren't useful to the real estate salespeople who would be using this page. To do this, she clicked on **Content: Node operations bulk form** and then on the **Remove** link at the bottom of the **Configure** field modal that appeared. She repeated the removing of the field for the **Content: Type (Content Type)** and **(author) User: Name (Author)** fields. Lynn noted that the username field appeared to be the only field reference to the author entity, so she could delete the relationship later.

Moving on to **FILTER CRITERIA**, Lynn was a bit confused by the first two filters. When she clicked on **Content: Published status or admin user**, the description said **Filters out unpublished content if the current user cannot view it**. "This seems reasonable, let's keep this filter," she thought, and she clicked on **Cancel**. Next was **Content: Publishing status (grouped)**, an exposed filter that lets the user filter by either published or unpublished. This seemed useful, so Lynn kept it and clicked on **Cancel**. The next filter, **Content: Type (exposed)**, is necessary but shouldn't be selectable by the user, so Lynn clicked on it to edit the filter, unselected the **Expose this filter to visitors** option, and selected just the **Property** content type, making the filter only select content that are properties. The next filter, **Content: Title (exposed)**, is handy, so Lynn left it as is. The final filter, **Content: Translation language (exposed)**, isn't needed as Lynn's site isn't multilingual, so Lynn deleted the filter.

Moving on to the center column of the view edit page, under the **PAGE SETTINGS** heading, Lynn changed the path for the view to /admin/property-maintenance by clicking on the existing /admin/content/node path, making the change, and clicking on the **Apply** button.

Next in this column was the menu setting. Lynn doesn't want the property maintenance page to be part of the administration content page, so she clicked on **Tab: Content** and changed the menu type to **Normal** menu entry. This changed the fields displayed on the right-hand side of the modal, so Lynn changed the **Menu** link title to **Property Maintenance**, left the description blank, and left **Show as expanded** unselected. In the **Parent** pull-down menu, she selected the **<Tools>** menu.

 Tools is the default Drupal menu for site tools that is only shown to authorized users, who are logged into the site, and can view the page linked to, which real estate salespeople will be able to view.

She left the weight at **-10**, planning on reorganizing this menu when she has most of it configured. As this is the last option, she clicked on **Apply** to exit the modal.

The last setting in the **PAGE SETTINGS** section is **Access**. Lynn knew she needed to change the required permission as she didn't plan on giving real estate salespeople access to the main content page, but she wasn't sure which permission to give them. Looking through the permissions page (the **People | Permissions** tab), Lynn didn't see any permissions that made sense for who should be able to see this maintenance page. So, she clicked on the **Permission** link in the center column of the view edit page and changed the **Access** value from **Permission** to **Role**, and when she clicked on the **Apply (all displays)** button, she could select the role(s) she wanted to be able to see on this page. She selected the **Administrator, Real Estate Salesperson**, and **Office Administrator** roles.

One way to test access while you develop is to use a second browser and log in as the other kind of user. A common mistake in Drupal is to see content while logged in as an administrator that can't be seen by other users. This can also be done using a second tab opened in "incognito" mode, but I find it easier to use a different browser (for example, Chrome and Firefox). You can even have three browsers open to the same page to test a third kind of user.

Continuing down the column, Lynn decided she didn't need a header or footer on this administration page at least for now, but she did want to change the **NO RESULTS BEHAVIOR** message. Drupal has a text message defined, so she clicked on the **Global: Unfiltered text (Global: Unfiltered text)** link, changed the **Content** field to **No properties meeting your filter criteria are available.**, and clicked on the **Apply (all displays)** button.

The final section, **PAGER**, seemed fine, so Lynn skipped over it and moved to the third column of the view edit page, **ADVANCED SETTINGS**. As Lynn had changed the setting to always show the advanced settings, Lynn noticed that there was a relationship for author. As she had deleted displaying the author name, there wasn't any reason to keep the relationship because she wasn't using any of the author's details. She clicked on the **author** link and then on the **Remove** link at the bottom of the modal. Reviewing the results of the live preview, Lynn was satisfied and clicked on the **Save** button to save her modified view.

There is a maxim in computers, *Save Early, Save Often*. As you develop or modify your view, when you reach a point where your progress so far is okay, click on the **Save** button. Then, if you make a terrible mistake in the next change, you can click on the **Cancel** button and then click on **Edit** to resume from where you last saved.

Before saving the view, the result looked similar to the following screen:

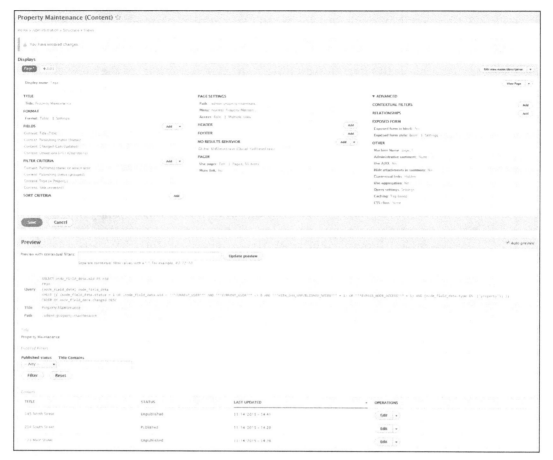

The resulting Property Maintenance view edit screen with all the changes

Debugging – Live Preview is your friend

Assuming you enabled Live Preview in your Views settings earlier in the chapter, as you are building your view, Views will show what will be displayed. Formatting and some JavaScript displays, such as Google mapping, can't be displayed in Live Preview, but to debug, you generally don't need them.

Many views' challenges are getting the data that you want to display or getting data to be displayed the way you want. Many views are created using the fields content display. Often, you will see fields that you don't want displayed when reviewing Live Preview because you didn't check the **Exclude from display** option in the field configuration. Or, you will select a field from the **Add fields** list that isn't actually the field you want to display the data you want—for instance, do you want **article tags** or **article tags (field_tags: delta)**? Sometimes you have to just try one and see what happens. If it isn't the right option, delete the field and try another. Experience will guide you as you use Views, but even the most experienced site builders wonder what some field or field option does in the context of the view they are building.

Remember to save the view before you experiment with this next idea. Then, if it doesn't work out, you can just click on **Cancel** and not lose all the previous work you put in.

If you disabled Live Preview, hopefully, you have decided to go back and enable it; seeing the output and looking at the generated SQL queries is really very useful in trying to figure out what might be going wrong.

"Okay, Jackson, I see that a lot of what I knew from the previous versions of Views applies to the version in Drupal 8. Now that I've quickly gone through the edit screen to modify a core view, let's get serious and really learn the ins and outs of this version of Views."

Summary

In this chapter we covered the Views administration page, where you can add, delete, edit, and duplicate views. Then, we reviewed all the general Views module settings. Finally, we modified a core view, quickly going through several configuration options, which will be covered in more detail in the rest of the book. If you have used Views in older versions of Drupal, you should feel comfortable. If this is your first introduction to Views, don't panic that we glossed over a lot or if you felt lost. We'll come back in later chapters and go through the entire Views edit page in much more detail.

In the next chapter, we'll start the in-depth exploration of Views, beginning with building a simple property listing that most real estate sites might have. This listing will get successive refinements in later chapters to make it very powerful, but for now, it is a simple list. This will lead to defining some Views terms, such as View Types, displays, Display Formats, and Display Contents. With the terminology established, we'll end with an interesting view that displays selected events from Drupal's Watchdog log to users that might normally not be able to see them.

2
Views from Scratch

In this chapter, we'll cover the basics of building Drupal Views. After building a simple listing of available properties, we will look at some Views terminology that defines the components of a view:

- Views types
- Displays
- Display Formats
- Display Contents

Finally, we'll finish the chapter by building a view from Drupal's watchdog log, which is something new in Drupal 8.

A first try at listing the available properties

"Okay, Jackson, we've modified an existing view. I think it's time to learn how to build my own views in Drupal 8." Lynn gave Jackson a nice scratch knowing she'd be ignoring him for a few hours while she worked her way through this first view on her own.

Starting at the Views listing page (**Manage | Structure | Views**), Lynn clicked on the **Add new view** button that is prominently at the top of the Views listing page. "This is a nice change from Drupal 7, where adding a view was just an unformatted link." After the page loaded, Lynn faced an empty form similar to the one here:

The blank Add new view screen

"Okay, this doesn't look too complex. Let's call this view *Available Property Listing*," said Lynn, as she typed the view name into the first field. Drupal automatically converts the name entered into this field into a machine name for Drupal to use internally.

Generally, the machine name generated by Drupal is fine, but if you want to change it, perhaps to add your own naming standards, you would click on the **Edit** link next to the machine name.

Adding a new view

"Jim said I should always add a description, so I'll check the **Description** checkbox." When she did, another field to hold the description appeared on the screen. "Okay, Jackson, I have a feeling that this simple form might be more complex than it appears when it first loads."

Moving to the **View Settings** fieldset, Lynn knew she wanted a view of real estate properties, so she selected the default **Content** option from the **Show selection** list. She only wanted to show properties, so she selected the **Property** option from the **of type** selection list. When she made this selection, the **tagged with** field disappeared. "Look Jackson, not every change adds more fields to fill out; some changes actually remove fields." Jackson didn't seem impressed by this observation, as he was sleeping. For the final selection of the fieldset, Lynn selected **sorted by Newest first**, figuring that most visitors would be interested in the latest properties for sale. "Fortunately, I can change most of these options later."

There were three more fieldsets, labeled **PAGE SETTINGS**, **BLOCK SETTINGS**, and **REST EXPORT SETTINGS**. Lynn wants a page with a table of properties, so she selected the **Create a page** checkbox and left the other two options blank.

New page settings

Selecting the **Create a page** option displayed a number of additional fields, which is required for Views to intelligently configure a page display. Here's what she did:

- For **Page title**, she left the default **Available Property Listing** title as is because it seemed like a reasonable title for the page.

- For **Path**, she again left the default **available-property-listing** path as is because it was a reasonable URL for the page, being aware that search engines like descriptive path names in URLs.

- In the **PAGE DISPLAY SETTINGS** fieldset, she selected the **Table** selection option. When she did, the other options disappeared, and **fields** was displayed in their place. Had she selected another option, such as an unformatted list, she would have to pick between titles, teasers, full content, or fields.

 When in doubt for a content display type, select fields; it is the most general of them, unless you know all you want is a list of teasers. Selecting fields will give you a default list of titles, but with the flexibility of adding more fields to be displayed.

- For **Items to display**, she changed the value from the default 10 items at a time to 5 items at a time as she didn't have a lot of sample data.

- She left the **Use a pager** checkbox selected, so Drupal would automatically add navigation options to the bottom of her table to see the many, many listings that would eventually be part of the site.

- Lynn checked the **Create a menu link** checkbox to add this page to Drupal's menu system. She could have left this blank and added the link using the menu maintenance page (**Manage | Structure | Menus**), but this keeps the menu information with the view.

- From the **Menu** selection pull-down, she picked **Main navigation** to have the page appear on the site's main menu, which is displayed on every page, along with the home link.

- For **Link text**, she entered more casual text: `What's for Sale`.

- Lynn wasn't sure whether to check the **Include RSS feed** option. "I know what an RSS feed is; I get most of my real estate news from my RSS feed, so I guess people might want to subscribe to new listings and get them in their RSS reader," she thought, and so she selected the option.

- She left **Feed path** at `available-property-listing.xml`, which is the default, as she didn't think it mattered what this path is.

- Finally, she left **Feed row style** at **content**, which is the default, not knowing what it really should be, and made a note to ask Jim about that someday.

Before clicking on the **Save and edit** button, the completed form looked similar to the following one:

The completed Add new view screen

She clicked on the **Save and edit** button and saw the view edit screen Views had generated, which looked similar to the following:

The View edit screen before any changes

"Okay, I've got a list of addresses. What other information should I display in my list of available properties? I need enough so that someone can see what's available, but not so much that they get overwhelmed." Lynn thought for a few minutes and decided to add the asking price, number of bedrooms, square footage, and neighborhood. These were the usual first questions that buyers had about any house she showed them.

Adding fields

She clicked on the **Add** button next to the **Fields** label, which displayed a list of the available fields she could add. There were over 100 fields, which felt overwhelming. Lynn used the search field and entered `asking`, which displayed **Property Asking Price**. She selected the **field** checkbox and clicked on the **Apply (all displays)** button. The **Configure field: Content: Property Asking Price** modal appeared. She scanned the options and decided that mostly they looked okay. She changed the label text to **Asking Price** and selected a comma thousand marker. She clicked on the **Apply (all displays)** button.

She then repeated the process for the number of bedrooms, entering `bedrooms` in the search field after clicking on **Add**. She selected **Property Number Bedrooms** and clicked on **Apply (all displays)**. She changed the label to **# Bedrooms**, didn't add a thousands separator, and clicked on **Apply (all displays)**. "I'd love to see the house that has that many bedrooms."

Next was square footage; she clicked on **Add** and typed `square` in the search field. Nothing came up. "Hmm, I wonder if I forgot to add a field for square footage," she thought. She opened another tab and went to the **Manage fields** tab of the Property content type. "Sure enough, I forgot to add this field," she realized and proceeded to add the field to her Property content type. She made a note saying she'd have to go back and edit all the existing properties to include a square footage.

She had left the field selection modal open while she added the new field in another tab and noticed that the field hadn't appeared in the modal. She clicked on **Cancel** and then on **Add** again and entered `square` in the search field. **Property Square Footage** appeared this time, and she selected it and clicked on **Apply (all displays)**. She set the field options to the same as the asking price, changing the label to **Square Feet**. As she had just set up the field with the suffix **sq ft**, she also noticed that the checkbox labeled **Display prefix and suffix** was selected by default.

"One last field," Lynn commented as she clicked on **Add** for the last time. Adding **Property Neighborhood**, she changed the label to just **Neighborhood**. When she got to the **Formatter** selection, she was confused by the **Label** option being selected. As none of the other options looked right either, she decided to let Views select for her. The result was what she wanted: the neighborhood of the listing. This seemed odd, but then she remembered that she had used taxonomy to select the neighborhood because it might change as Blue Ridge grew. The term Label wasn't intuitive, but it was obviously the taxonomy term title versus the term ID stored in the entity reference.

Lynn decided the preview looked reasonable and clicked on **Save** to save the view.

The anatomy of a view

Lynn was confused a couple of times as she built her first view of available properties, so she decided that an hour with Jim would be really handy. Calling Jim, she said "Hi Jim, I just built my first view on the development site."

"Congratulations! That's a big step forward," he replied.

"However, I found it really confusing. There are so many options, and the terminology is so different from anything I've worked with before. I wonder whether you would have some time soon to sort of walk me through some of what I saw. I have a feeling if I master some of this terminology, the rest will fall into place."

"Drupal does have its own unique language. Some words don't exist anywhere else, and others have different meanings from what you might be used to hearing. I agree a quick rundown would be handy. Do you have a free hour some evening this week?"

Jim and Lynn decided to meet at a local Starbucks on Tuesday evening while Lynn's son was taking his Kung Fu class. On Tuesday, Lynn came in, got a coffee, and waited for Jim, who arrived a couple of minutes later. After Lynn bought him the coffee she owed him, they sat at a table near the front window that had power nearby so that they could plug in their computers.

"If you can learn a few terms and what the options for these terms mean, you'll really know how to approach building views in Drupal," Jim started out. "Let's look at the four major terms you saw while building your first view." Jim had a pad of paper in addition to his computer and wrote down the following list:

- View Types
- Displays
- Display formats
- Display contents

"Let's talk through each one in this order." Jim then launched into teaching mode and Lynn listened intently.

View Types

"View Types are a way to say what Views is making lists of (or whatever Display Format you are building). You can think of View Type as the kind of information that you can use to build a list or, using computer speak, query.

You can only have one View Type for a given view, a lot like trying to mix a dog or cat with wild animals in a cage. The unexpected is most likely to result. When you think of it, this makes sense. It wouldn't make sense to have a property listing that also included the names of your realtors mixed in as if they were properties.

That isn't to say you can't have information from two different content types in the same view. You can, and this is typically done with the relationships you defined in your content type definitions. I saw that on your development site, you have relationships between properties, owners, and realtors and a relationship between open houses and properties.

Relationships can actually go more than one level. Consider the fact that you have a relationship between an open house and a property; you can use the relationship between properties and realtors to know the first name of the realtor responsible for an open house.

Picking the right View Type is actually important because of relationships. Relationships are mostly one directional. So, if you have a View Type of an open house, you can have a relationship to a property, and Drupal knows how to make the related data available to you. Views can do a reverse relationship lookup, but you really want to make every effort to get the View Type set up right because working backwards puts a big strain on your database. If you saw the generated SQL queries option turned on, you'd see how much more complex these queries become, so my advice is to start with the right View Type. Generally, you will use the type that has references to other entities rather than the type that has references to it. As an example, if you wanted to combine open houses with properties, you should start with the open house content View Type and then add the property content as a relationship. When you get into relationships later, you'll see how this all fits together.

 Picking the right View Type or content selection within the content View Type can mean the difference between easily building a view and making it difficult, if not impossible, to build once you have relationships. If you find you are having a hard time finding the content you want, you might want to reconsider which content type you started with.

This brings up a pair of terms I forgot. You are familiar with the content you create when you add content. In Drupalspeak, these are called nodes. Nodes have been part of Drupal since the very first version. When the CCK module was written for Drupal 5, they became much more flexible, and CCK's functionality was included in Drupal 7 much the same way Views is included in Drupal 8.

Drupal 7 also introduced a much more powerful concept: entities. Nodes are entities, but so are all sorts of other things. Users and taxonomy terms were entities in Drupal 7. There were some things that didn't make it into entities in Drupal 7, such as files. Now, everything in Drupal 8 is an entity. A nice part of this complete conversion is that Views can use any entity as a View Type, even the internal Drupal watchdog logs that track what is going on in your site, such as when people log in, add or edit content, or install new modules. The watchdog logs also keep a record of various errors, such as a missing file. But I'm getting side tracked; let's go back to View Types.

Drupal core defines a number of View Types; contributed modules can have additional types, especially if they have data that isn't stored as content.

Content

Content is, by far and away, the most commonly used View Type. I would go as far as saying that 95% of all of the views I ever created were content views. Most websites are defined by the content their owners create. That's why, when you create a new view, it defaults to being a content View Type.

You use a content View Type when you make a list of the most recent posts on your blog, or for that matter, the main blog display page. You also use a content View Type when you create a slideshow using a dedicated content type or fields from an existing content type. Even most Google Maps displayed by Drupal are views of content.

Even though you may have many different content types defined on your site, you have four custom and two default ones from a standard installation; all content is created equal, as far as Views is concerned. This can produce results that are incomplete, as views just puts an empty value in the place of missing content, which could happen if you combined, say, properties and owners. They have very few fields that are the same.

Even if your content types look as though they have the same fields, such as your property owner and realtor content types, if the fields aren't the same (in other words, they aren't shared fields), you won't get the information from one content type or the other on any given line because you selected a field that only appears in one or the other content types.

While I don't generally recommend using shared fields, if you do have a use case where you need two different content types that will be displayed together in a single view and need to display this field from either content type, it might make sense to use a shared field. There are ways to combine two fields that will become apparent when you get around to discovering field rewrites later.

Remember I said that to Views, all content is created equal? Generally, you don't want to mix your content types together; an exception is the nice content listing page that is built into Drupal core. The way you select only a single content type is by adding a filter. This use case is so common that, when you create a content View Type, you get a selection option to pick which content type you want to select. While you may think that this is actually defining separate View Types for each content type, in reality, it is a single View Type—content—and an automatically generated filter.

Content revisions

If you check the **Create new revision** option in the publishing options tab when you create or edit content, Drupal will save a copy of the previous version of the node and keep track of it.

> I like to change the default setting for the **Create new revision** field in the content type when I create new types so that Drupal will default to keeping the revisions. Then, if a content editor messes up and accidentally deletes a big chunk of content from a node, recovering is as simple as reverting back to the version that was saved in the revision.

Generally, when you create a view of content, all you are able to display is the current revision of any content included in this view. If you were to create a view that required the previous revisions—say, to show how a piece of content has changed over time—you'd need to create a view of content revisions. An example of this kind of view would be Wikipedia's **View history** tab, which shows up on each page and displays the various edits to this page, who made them, and when.

To be honest, I've never built a view of content revisions.

Comments

I have to say, in general, I hate comments on most websites. They are spam content magnets and take a lot of the site owner's time to administer, or you end up with a cesspool of trash associated with your content.

However, if you do want to have comments, they are now entities in themselves. This means that you could add a module, such as five stars, and let other visitors vote on how useful a given comment is. Then, using Views, you could create a list of the most popular comments in your system, regardless of what content they appear on.

Log entries

This is a new View Type in Drupal 8, and it looks interesting. Before Drupal 8, you'd have to give a user more administrative permissions to let them see the Drupal Watchdog log. Also, you'd have to show them how to use the filters, which were pretty well hidden. This generally leaves monitoring the logs to the developers.

One of the most common issues with any website is a broken link, either within the site because of some change, or from the outside; perhaps, the other website might get the wrong URL. If the broken link is from your website, you'd want to fix it. If it is an external site with a bad URL, you might want to use the redirect module to forward traffic to the correct page.

With the ability to create a view of log entries, you can have a page or block that displays the recent 404 or "file not found" errors that you can let users without full administrative access to the site use to see the broken links.

One limitation of this View Type is that you need to have Drupal's database logging module enabled. Many sites turn this module off in production to reduce the load on the database server and replace it with the syslog module, which writes the same information into the server's Apache log. When the database module is uninstalled, the log entries View Type disappears. Any defined views are deleted and don't come back if the module is re-enabled. Make sure you have saved a copy of those views via configuration management before uninstalling the database logging module.

Files

Every file uploaded in a file field is tracked by Drupal, which includes image fields that are a special variant of the file field. Part of this tracking is to know when it is safe to delete the file. For example, a file may be uploaded as part of one content type but referenced by others; the original content may be deleted, and you may not want the file to be deleted yet because it is used until the last bit of content that uses the file is deleted. Then, and only then, should the file be removed from the server so that extra files don't hang around and take server space.

Most of the views you might build will most likely be administrative views to manage the content that gets uploaded, although it might be possible that you want to have a view on your site that shows visitors every PDF file that is uploaded and available via the site. I would guess such a view on the IRS site would be thousands of pages long. But a more likely use might be to populate a selected list of images that could be used in the content.

Taxonomy terms

While taxonomy terms are frequently used to filter your views, depending on whether you added fields to your taxonomy terms or even used the taxonomy description/body field that Drupal adds by default, it is possible that you would want to create views to display this additional information. Many sites use taxonomy terms as additional content types storing all sorts of supplementary data in the taxonomy term. This data needs to be displayed, and much like views of content, views of taxonomy terms are needed.

Coupled with the entity reference display type, you can use views of taxonomy terms to populate select lists or autocomplete on the content entry/edit forms. As an example, you might have two taxonomies attached to a given content type. Depending on the value of the first—say, some category taxonomy—you might want to limit the options in another field. This other field would be configured to use a widget that is a view filtered by the option selected in the first taxonomy field. Now, it will be possible to make it harder for content editors to select the wrong options—a definite plus for Drupal 8!

Users

After content—the clear number one—and taxonomy terms, the most used View Type in Drupal 7 was probably users. Lists of users have been part of Drupal since the early versions. Things such as who's logged in or the most recent visitors are interesting information on sites where users have accounts and can log in; or intranets and social sites, such as the travel agency down the street where users share travel experiences on a forum and can set up blogs to describe their trips while they travel.

Due to the fact that users can have fields as they are entities, just like in Drupal 7, there is additional information that has likely been stored as part of a user that you might want to display. Often in sites, users can't add or edit content beyond, say, a blog post, forum post, or comment, but there are several fields of information about themselves that they are encouraged to fill out. Views of this information are often used to display more about the author on pages related to them.

Custom blocks

This is another new View Type in Drupal 8. Not only can you define custom blocks in Drupal 8 and place them anywhere, they can have fields, which wasn't possible in Drupal 7 unless you used a contributed module such as Bean. Again, any time you have fields on some entity, there will likely be a need to be able to display these fields or use them to sort or select. I noticed that there are a number of predefined operation fields for custom blocks, so one use would be to have a view that lets you manage the blocks that a particular content editor should be able to manage. They might need to be able to update an alert banner block that is normally empty and not displayed, but not be able to update the block that contains some part of your site branding. This can be accomplished using a custom blocks View Type.

Custom block revisions

This is another new View Type in Drupal 8. Similar to content revisions, a view of custom block revisions could be built to show how a block changes as it is edited. For instance, a custom block view might include a view showing the dates and revision log entries for the last five versions before the current version. I'm sure as Drupal 8 is in the field longer, some good examples using this View Type will show up in the blogosphere; until then, just know that it is possible.

Other View Types

Modules can define additional View Types. Drupal core's Log Entries View Type isn't part of the Views module but rather of the Database Logging (dblog) module. Other contributed modules will likely provide additional View Types when they are enabled, especially if they add data to your site that isn't part of an existing entity. Don't be surprised to find new View Types with each module addition, and think about how they can be used if the module doesn't include any view definitions.

Okay, I think we have beaten View Types to death, so let's move on to the next major part of a view: Displays.

Displays

Displays are the highest level of how Views "display" your results. Notice that I used air quotes around the word "display" because most of the displays created by Views aren't actually displayed in the traditional sense.

The best way to think of a display is that it is the way Drupal packages your results. While you probably think that all views result in a standalone page, many views on Drupal sites are actually blocks inserted on the page by the theme. Other displays might generate code that is used by other websites, or allow Drupal developers to use the result of a view as part of their custom code.

A lot of Views newbies overload a single view with bunches and bunches of displays. Some are simple variants of others because the view creator probably didn't understand how to make a contextual filter work (or even know what they are). If you find yourself creating a new display and only changing the value of a filter, ask yourself if there is a way to have this filter work with the information already available; if so, use a contextual filter and a single display.

At other times, each display is so different from the other displays that they are really different views. I don't think it is a good idea to put a blog listing, the most recent posts, and most popular posts in the same view. How you build each one is different enough that putting them in their own views will make it easier to make changes to one and not impact the others.

My rule of thumb is that unless the displays are basically the same, you are better off cloning the view and creating another dedicated view than adding an unrelated display. This keeps your views simple and modular, which is important if you want to export them to another site using the Features module. If you have more than a half dozen changes from display to display, they are no longer basically the same; but again, this is just a general guideline. The basic goal is to keep each view simple and discrete.

Remember that it is easy to accidentally change the other displays in your view if you forget to change the **For** option from **All displays** to **This page (override)**! I can't tell you how many times I've made this mistake while making a change in a hurry, only to have the client call a couple of days later when the other display doesn't work the way it used to.

A common reason to have two displays is if you want to display more or less the same information on a standalone page, using a page display, and in a block, using a block display. The page display might have some additional details versus the block, which might be a simple unformatted list of titles. However, the rest of the logic, filtering, sorting, relationships, and so on, are all the same, so it makes sense to have both the displays in the same view.

Master

Depending on how you have your Views settings configured, if you create views that start with a page or block display, you might never see the master display, although it is always there. You can configure Views to always show it, which may have some use or be a confusing addition. I generally leave the setting at the default option of not always showing the master display.

Assuming the default setting, if you create a new view and don't specify any other display before clicking on the **Save and edit** button, you will only see the master display. Then, on the view edit page, as soon as you add a display, the master display will disappear.

Where having the master display show is handy is when you have two or three displays and want to make a change to all of them. While in theory you can edit any of the displays and update the others by making sure the **For** option is selected to **All displays,** for some people, it makes more sense to edit the master display. So, whether or not you choose to display the master display is purely a matter of preference. Remember that if a given display overrides a setting, even changing the master display won't change it back.

Page

A common view display is the page display. If you are looking at a page on a Drupal site that appears to be a list, there is a good chance that it is a page display of a view creating this list. If it isn't, the site builder messed up, because content editors really shouldn't have to maintain lists of other content on a Drupal site.

Page displays generate all the HTML for a standalone page. In most themes, these pages all have a common structure, such as the heading, footers, or sidebar regions, and the page display just generates the content block. As Drupal 8 treats the content as a block anyway, the difference between a page and block display isn't as great as in the previous versions of Drupal.

One other difference between a page display and a block display is that you can assign a URL to a page display and put a link to a views-generated page in a menu, both as part of the view in the center column of the edit page.

Block

The other common view display is a block; if counted separately, there are probably more block views than page views. As an example, you might have a blog post page view and then define several block views, such as recent posts, related posts, or the most popular posts.

The block view display defines a block to which you can give a specific name in the center column of the edit page, which can be placed anywhere in your theme using Drupal's block interface or if you use some other contributed module, such as Panels or Context, via their interface. Given that you can insert the same block more than once on a page, in theory, you could have the same view block appear in a couple places, and through the creative use of contextual filters, you can actually have very different results displayed in each block.

Blocks are much more flexible in where they can be placed on a page. However, many of the regions you might put a block in are much narrower than the content region, so some display options, such as using a pager or defining a table in a block, might not make as much sense as in the content area of a page display.

Attachment

Attachments are very powerful, and most Drupal site builders don't even know they are there.

An attachment display is what its name says it is: a view display that is attached to another view display. As an example, say you wanted a block with a list of the five latest properties listed with the agency. This is easy in views. However, what if you wanted to include the featured image of the most recent listing in the same block?

You could do this with an attachment display. You'd create the view with the block you want, and then you'd add another display that's an attachment. This display can have its own fields by overriding the original display's list; in this case, it would be a single field with the featured image formatted as a thumbnail.

> As you get better with Views, if you planned out your view in advance, you'd know you were going to override the other display and would likely create the first display as overridden to start with. This keeps the field list of the original display separate from any additional displays. This becomes more important if you want to get really creative with each display's configuration.

Part of the configuration of an attachment display is whether to display it before or after the content displayed by the attached display. Selecting before would add this second display to the block created by the view. If this second display were defined to display a single thumbnail image, the block would look similar to an image followed by a list of five addresses.

With entity reference fields as part of the Drupal 8 core, the possibilities become even more interesting. Virtually every part of a view can be overridden, with the exception of the View Type, which is the type of information being displayed. However, since most views are displays of content, also known as nodes, you can mix several different types of data together in a single page or block.

For example, say you had a view that displayed the latest five properties again but on a page. You can define an attachment display that used the relationship between the properties and the open house content type to pull in the open houses from the same properties. You could then build a view that used only the open house fields to display a list of open houses and have it automatically displayed below the list of properties.

You can even share contextual filters and exposed filters between the two displays, letting them act as if they were a single, very complex view.

Attachments are so powerful and flexible that when they were introduced in the Drupal 6 version of Views, someone wrote a 300-page book just on Views attachments.

Embed

This is a new display included in Views for Drupal 8 that is mostly of interest to developers, as it is used to embed the Views output in pages using PHP via the `views_embed_view()` function.

This capability existed in Drupal 7, just not quite as visibly. Sometimes, it was used in custom code to create a block that used arguments that couldn't be figured out using the built-in contextual filter tricks.

Generally, you won't be interested in these displays, although it is possible that you might end up editing one. Just remember that the results are used by some custom code, so make sure you check with the developer before making changes that impact an embed display.

It isn't completely clear what function the embed display will perform in Drupal 8. It appears that `views_embed_view()` still allows embedding any display associated with the view. Also, as of writing this book, there is a lack of any documentation on how it should work, and the embed display is an empty class definition with the comment *This display plugin does nothing apart from exist*. I do like the idea of using this display as a signal to site builders that the view is being used by code. It is possible that in the future releases of Drupal 8, the function might require an embed display to insert a view display via code.

Entity reference

This is a new display included in Views for Drupal 8 that really excites me.

When you created the reference fields in your content type, the default entry widget was an autocomplete field. As you type part of the referenced entity title, Drupal will start to display a list of options. When you see the one you want, you can use your mouse to select it, and Drupal will convert this title into a reference, which is typically a number that uniquely references what you are referring to (a node ID, or **nid**, in the case of content, and a taxonomy ID, or **tid**, in the case of taxonomy terms, and so on).

Imagine you have a lot of content on your site—say 10,000 nodes. This makes the list pretty long until you have typed most or all of the title. This is a pain for your content editors.

Worse, a simple node reference would display not only properties, but realtors, owners, and random pages. This is one reason that Drupal lets you specify what content types can be included in a reference. The content type is used to limit the options that exist in this field.

But this could still be a long list. On your current site, you have 10,000 properties, but only a few hundred are actually for sale. So, even limiting a reference field to only the property type would result in most of the content being on the site. Also, as you know on your current site, it is too easy to accidentally select a property that isn't for sale any more.

Now, with the entity reference View Type you can define a view of properties with a filter that only includes properties that are for sale. Save the view so that you can manage fields for the content type, say open houses. Then, edit the field that references the property content type. Now, instead of the default reference type that lets you specify which content types and sort order to use, you can select the view you just created. So now, when you start to type a title in the autocomplete field when entering or editing an open house, instead of all the properties that start with what you've typed, you will only see properties that are for sale.

Another way to use this option is selecting an entity by something other than its title. Just define the entity reference View Type with the field that makes sense; it probably should be unique so that you can select the right option, and you can select by, say, the telephone number of the owner.

Feed

Every Drupal site has a predefined RSS feed that can be accessed via the URL yoursite.com/rss.xml. However, it has limited configuration options (the number of items, feed description, and whether to include full content, title, or teasers). Each content type can define a custom RSS feed display mode. However, the feed only includes content that is configured with the **Promote to front page** option, and there is only the one feed for the site.

For many sites, you might have blogs configured that don't promote any content to the site front page but have one or more blog displays configured instead as secondary landing pages. In fact, on many sites, adding content with the **Promote to front page** option set would cause content to appear on the site's front page that isn't supposed to be there. However, blogs really should have an RSS feed so that readers can subscribe to the blog and get updates directly in their RSS readers when new posts are published.

 If all you want is a feed without any other display, such as a page or block that is generated by the **Add view** dialog, getting it set up seems confusing. When you add the view, don't select any of the three displays included on the **Add new feed** page. Then, when you click on the **Add and edit** button, you'll only see the master or default display on the view edit screen. Once at the view edit screen, you can add the feed display and have a view that only has the feed without any other displays.

Alternatively, you might want to have a feed for a certain type of content that isn't blogging. For example, if you had a store on your site, you might create a feed of new products that your customers could subscribe to. Then, when you add a new product, they would be alerted via their RSS reader. For visitors that don't use an RSS reader, there are ways to incorporate RSS feed into most e-mail clients, such as Outlook in Microsoft.

 If you create a RSS feed for your site, make sure you put links to the feed prominently displayed on the corresponding pages (for a blog, I'd recommend both the feed overview and each blog post). There's nothing worse than finding a great blog and not being able to figure out how to subscribe to it. I'd even put the RSS feed links at both the top and bottom of each page so that they are easy to find and use.

REST export

This is a new display in Drupal 8 now that it has web services built into the core. You do need to have the RESTful Web Services module enabled for this option to appear.

 Web services provide you with the ability to share your data with other applications or websites. While Drupal has long had the ability to have RSS feed with information, web services is much more flexible and allows not only sharing data but also another application or website to actually update data inside Drupal. This kind of data sharing is often called an API, or application programming interface, and more and more websites have APIs for their data. Having web services is a key requirement for using the newer JavaScript frameworks, such as Node.js and others, to replace Drupal's native frontend. This practice is often called "headless" or "decoupled" Drupal.

Drupal's basic web services allow an application to read or write a single content type via a URL plus some additional information passed through the HTTP headers. The **REST Export** option in Views extends this basic API to allow you to do everything that Views offers, to mix and match data from several different content types, users, and so on and then make it available as a single API.

In addition, you can use contextual filters with your REST export views, the value is passed via the URL, just as if you were using a contextual filter for a page or block. This gives any API you define using this View display a lot of power to return just what the application calling it needs.

You can select whether the response will allow JSON, XML, or HAL JSON.

 For REST exports, the application can specify the format via the URL with the `?_FORMAT=JSON` (or `?_FORMAT=XML` or `?_FORMAT=HAL_JSON`) parameter.

Display Formats

Once you have decided what you will output using a View Type and how you will output it using a display, you are ready to tell Views how to format the information you will output. Display formats show up on the Views edit screen in the **FORMAT** fieldset, as shown here:

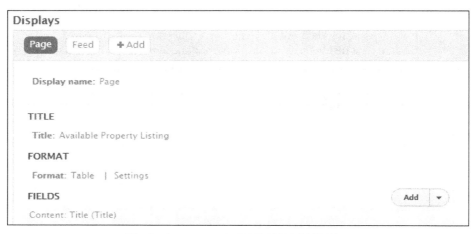

Display formats are the FORMAT field/fieldset

Display formats are the layout options that are wrapped around the individual groups or rows of a view's output. When combined with CSS provided by the core or your theme, they can accomplish amazing transformations. Later, when we look at add-on modules for Views, you will see that not only can Views generate lists and tables, it can generate slideshow carousels, maps, and other displays.

Out of the box, Drupal 8 only has four Display formats, but add-on modules can add many more useful Display formats. In fact, you'll notice that the Geolocation module you added to the site to allow you to add longitude and latitude to your property listings also added a Views Display Format of **Geolocation – CommonMap**.

Even after you select a Display Format, you can change it later by clicking on the **Format** name link under the **FORMAT** options in the first column of the view edit screen. If you clicked on **Table** in the previous example screen, you'd see this:

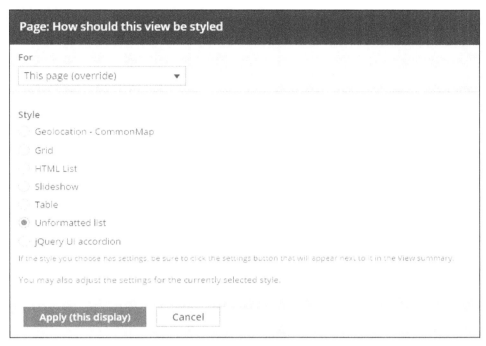

Display format options, including some from contributed modules

With a few exceptions, such as Google maps, which are generated via JavaScript, when you make a change, you will see the general results in your preview area. Do remember that the previews are formatted using the administration theme, which may mean that some of your custom CSS formatting won't show in the preview. If you don't like the Display Format you selected, you can always click on **Cancel** and ignore all your changes since the last time you saved your view. This is handy because sometimes, you don't know which format will generate better HTML for your application, and being able to try several options before committing to one is handy.

The unformatted list

The simplest of the Display Formats is the **Unformatted list** option. Views simply output your fields one after another without adding any structure to the output, except some divs that contain formatting classes. This Display Format can be very useful if you want straight output or can manipulate the classes output the way you want with CSS.

The HTML list

Adding just a little structure to the unformatted list Display Format is done with the **HTML List** option. The output is virtually the same, except that it is wrapped in either the <UL> or <OL> tags, and each row is wrapped in <LI> tags. The result, if all you output is titles, is either a numbered list or a list of bullet points, which is determined by one of the Display Format options that you can select after choosing the **HTML List** option or later by selecting the **Settings** link next to the **HTML List** link.

Grid

Moving into two dimensions, the **Grid** Display Format outputs your view results in a two-dimensional grid. Settings for the **Grid** Display Format include the number of columns and whether the table is organized horizontally (that is, each group of output is output from left to right and then by starting from the left-hand side again when the last column is reached) or vertically (that is, each group of output is output until the number of rows necessary to hold the data being displayed is filled, and then the next column fills from top to bottom).

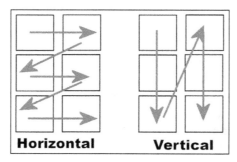

Grid layout options

Note that the HTML code generated for a **Grid** Display Format does not use HTML tables but relies on CSS formatting to create the grid display instead. This gives you a lot more flexibility to reformat via CSS for different devices.

You might want to be careful if you are displaying a fixed number of items or using the pager with a fixed number of items to make sure that the number is divisible by the number of columns. Otherwise, Views will happily leave the remainder of columns in the last row. As an example, the content listing view is set to display 50 items per page, displaying this as a grid in four columns will result in two items being displayed in the last row.

Table

The last built-in Display Format is **Table**. It is also very powerful and flexible. Also, it has the most options!

The **Table** Display Format gets a bit of a bad reputation because it generates HTML tables, which are more difficult to make responsive. They can be made responsive; it just takes more effort.

For this Display Format, it helps to be looking at the **Style options** modal, which looks similar to the one here:

Table Display Format style options

Within the style options of the **Table** Display Format is a large number of options. One option not in the style options is what order to display the fields in, which is determined by the order of the fields in the field section.

There is no requirement that if you have 10 fields that you want to display, then your table should have 10 columns. You can "fold" more than one field into a single column. In which column to display each field can be set in the first set of options for the **Table** Display Format. The columns are "named" by the labels of the fields they are defined by, so if you had a view with the fields Title, Asking Price, # Bedrooms, Square Footage, and Neighborhood, then the columns would be named with the same labels.

To combine # Bedrooms and Square Footage, you'd change one or the other field's column to be the same as the other. So, I might change # Bedrooms to be in the Square Footage column. This would combine the two values into the same column, and the other column options would apply to the pair of values, as shown here:

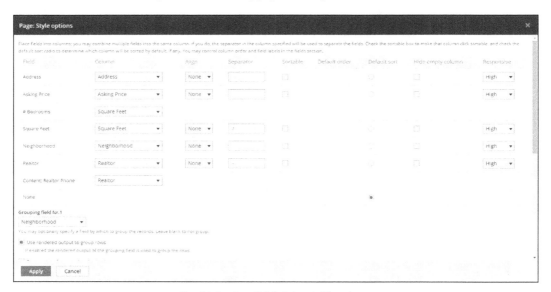

Combining two fields into a table column

The two values are simply concatenated with a space unless you specify a separator. This might make sense if you wanted to build a full name from a first name and last name field. However, most of the time, you'll want some kind of separator; in our case, a slash character makes sense.

Note that even though I specified the separator in the second field, when the two fields are combined, the order of fields determines the order within the column. If you wanted something similar to *lastname, firstname*, you would have to order the fields to have a *lastname* before the *firstname* and use a comma as the separator.

There is no limit to how many fields you can combine into a single column other than what makes sense.

Each column can be aligned independently of the other columns by selecting the appropriate alignment (left, right, or center) in the **ALIGN** column of options. The alignment not only changes how the data is displayed, but also how the column label is displayed.

Each column can be made sortable. If you select a column as **Sortable**, the column label is transformed into a link. Click on this link, and the view is rebuilt for the user using the selected column as a sort order. Using the example of your initial property list, changing this setting would let a visitor switch from displaying the most recent properties first to displaying the least expensive properties first. Changing the sort order of the table is remembered from page to page, so upon switching the order to price and going from the first to the second page, the list will still be by price and won't change back to the view defined on the last updated date. If you take a look at the URL, you'll notice that Views has added some parameters to let it know how the view is to be adapted: `?order=title&sort=asc`. This behavior assumes that the **Override normal sorting if click sorting is used** option is not unselected.

If you let columns be sortable, then a new option will appear for the default sort order: ascending or descending. In addition, you can specify which column should be the default column to sort by, effectively eliminating the sort options defined by display. If you specify none, a "column" is added at the end of the list of columns; then, the display's sort order will be used as a default.

The next column option is a **Hide empty column**. Some views will result in columns that don't have information based on the filters that are applied, usually exposed filters or contextual filters. This option will let you hide the whole column in these cases and not confuse your visitor.

The final column lets you tell Views how to adapt the table for mobile devices. Remember that Drupal 8 is responsive from the beginning, and tables can be problematic. So, views let you specify the priority of each column as high, medium, or low. As the view port gets narrower and Views runs out of space, the low priority columns are not displayed. If this isn't enough, the medium priority columns are dropped, leaving just the high priority columns. Obviously, this doesn't work if you don't change the Views default of all the columns being high priority. You can see this in the administrative views that come built into Drupal 8.

For a demonstration of how these settings operate, take a look at the short video at https://drupalize.me/blog/201409/ how-add-responsive-tables-content-drupal-8.

The next **Table** Display Format option is the **Grouping field Nr.1** (number one) option. Sometimes, you define a view that generates multiple rows with the same value. For example, in your view, the neighborhood might frequently be repeated as you have several properties in each neighborhood. Using the grouping field, you can combine all the properties with the same neighborhood into its own mini table with the labels repeated at the top. Usually, you have the same sort order as the grouping field, but this isn't a requirement. However, the grouping is done based on comparing the values of the field to the last row. So, if you sort by price and group by neighborhood, it is likely that each property will end up being its own group, unless two properties from the same neighborhood happen to follow each other in the listing by accident. If you are using a grouping field, you can specify whether the data or rendered output should be used for the comparison to group, which might result in different groups, depending on the formatting of the data.

The next two options change the CSS classes generated by Views for each row in the table. The first field lets you specify your own class to add to the table row div. The second option lets you disable the classes that Views adds to give a themer a lot of selection options. Many tables don't need this much flexibility, and it saves on the markup being output.

The next option, **Override normal sorting if click sorting is used**, can end up being confusing to visitors. It defaults to checked, which results in the behavior described previously. However, if you clear it, then click-sorting only works within the sort defined by the view. So, for your view, if the sort were set to the time of the last update and the default sort order, then click-sorting would appear to not operate.

The next option, **Enable Drupal style "sticky" table headers (Javascript)**, is handy if you define views with very long tables of lots of rows. Selecting this option will keep the column labels visible even if the top of the table scrolls off the top of the page. It is sort of similar in Excel, where you choose to lock the first row or two at the top of a page so that the column headings are always visible as you scroll through a spreadsheet.

The next option, **Caption for the table**, is part of Drupal 8's increased accessibility emphasis. You should give each table a caption that is made part of the HTML code of the table to let screen readers announce the purpose of the table and users skip a table full of information that they don't need to see. It is sort of similar to always adding the alt text to your images. The **Summary title** inside the **Table details** fieldset that follows is an additional accessibility option.

The final option, **Show the empty text in the table**, lets you force the table to be output even if the view has no results. Normally, if a view has no results, then none of the table HTML is output. You might use the HTML table in JavaScript and want it output or to debug.

Display Contents

Display Contents tell Views what to display. For some Display Formats, you don't have an option of what you can display. As an example, the **Table** Display Format we just discussed has to display fields. The other two Display Content options, content/entity or search results, would generate a disappointing table as each is really just a single presentation of the content being displayed. A table of just one column isn't much of a table, is it? However, other Display Formats, such as an unformatted list, lend themselves to the other Display Contents.

Fields

By far the most flexible, and I would say most commonly used Display Contents type, is fields. Selecting this display type will let you select exactly what part of the content or entity you want to display and gives you complete control over how it is displayed from inside the view. The other two Display Contents types, content and search results, display the content using other parts of Drupal's built-in rendering.

 As a general rule of thumb, if you aren't sure what kind of Display Contents type to select, pick fields. Almost always, this is what you'll end up using, especially if you need relationships or want to use field rewriting.

With the fields Display Contents type, you can select which fields to display. To add another field, click on the **Add** button to the right of the **Fields** fieldset label. When you add a field, a modal will be displayed with a large number of fields. Even if you do a view of basic pages, which only has to have two user entry fields, there are dozens of fields you can display via Views. Many of these fields are automatically maintained by Drupal, such as the date the content was last updated or the user ID of the person who created the content. Some fields are calculated by Views, such as **View result counter**, which displays the row number of the row being displayed. Other fields are added by various modules.

Note that if you try to delete all the fields from a fields Display Contents type, Views will display an error that there isn't any output selected. Even if you don't want the default field of **Title**, add your other fields to the view before deleting it.

When you create a view and select a Display Contents type, there are more options. Two of these are:

- Titles (linked)
- Titles

These automatically create a fields Display Contents and add the title field. In the first case, the field options are preset to link the title to its content, and in the second, they aren't. These options are just shortcuts for common, quick listings.

Content/entity

In the early days of Views, this Display Contents type would have simply been called node, as that's all the first version of Views could display. Then, by Drupal 7, it got a little more complex because nodes, other entities, and a few other View Types could be displayed using Views. Now that almost anything in Drupal 8 is an entity, it probably should be called an Entity Display Contents, but there are some new View Types that were added in Drupal 8 that don't use entities. These View Types are:

- Content revisions
- Custom block revisions
- Log entries

The View Types that don't use entities don't have a content/entity Display Content type.

The rest of the View Types have a content/entity Display Content type. Instead of calling it a display of content, the Display Content mirrors the View Type name. So, for content, the content/entity Display Content is labeled **Content**; for file, the content/entity Display Content is labeled **File**, and so on.

The content/entity Display Contents type uses Drupal's built-in rendering of the entity. How and what is displayed is determined by the display mode selected in the **Row style** options. Display modes are configured by the content type, and the configuration is managed in the **Manage display** tab of the content type definition (**Manage | Structure | Content Types**). Then, select the **Manage display** option for the content type you want to modify, or the **Manage display** tab if you are configuring some other aspect of the content type. You can also create additional display modes for each entity type by going to **Manage | Structure | Display modes**.

When you create a view and select a content Display Contents type, there are more options. Two of these options are:

- Teasers
- Full content

These automatically create a content/entity Display Contents and set the display mode to use. In the first option, the teaser display mode is used, and in the second, the full content display mode is selected. Note that there are other display modes that can be selected from the settings on the view edit page, especially if you create additional display modes (**Structure** | **Display modes** | **View modes**).

Views will render the content/entity being displayed using the display mode selected; so, you can insert this result into its display, usually wrapping the rendered output with its own formatting HTML.

Search results

The search results display is a bit of an enigma to me. From what I can tell, it may not be working, and there is an issue open for Drupal 8 about the problem at `https://www.drupal.org/node/2702291`. It looks as though the option might not have worked in the Drupal 7 version of Views either, and it's very likely that the option will be removed. So, if in a future version of Drupal you don't see it, this patch was committed.

However, from what I can tell from the code that is there, it would appear that if it were working, it would display search results, most likely using the search results view mode—the one defined in **Structure** | **Display modes** | **View modes** and not as part of Views. From what I can tell looking at the code, it would appear that to have anything useful come out of the view, you need a filter set to **Search: Search Keywords**. I guess this sort of makes sense; otherwise, the SQL query just looks like a standard views listing query. However, adding this field adds SQL joins to the search index tables and appears to use search results instead of content queries to generate which rows should be displayed. I actually set my filter to be exposed so that I could experiment with it easier. I got the search query part working by switching the display to **Content** and showed teasers. However, switching the display back to **Search Results** will show a pager, if the search keyword is really general or empty but nothing else. I also saw theme errors in the Drupal logs, so I suspect there's a theme template missing that no one has noticed. Obviously, this isn't a display that is used very much if Drupal 8 has been out as long as it has and nobody noticed this issue before. It did lead me to seeing the value of using the **Search: Search Keywords** filter with other displays, especially if you exchanged the built-in Drupal search with an external search, such as Solr.

This is a relatively comprehensive description of the anatomy and terminology of a View. If you were confused before, I'm not sure I didn't just make it worse with all the information I gave you in a short period of time."

"This has been a really valuable lecture on Views terminology and what the various options might be used for. I appreciate you having spent the time to go over it with me." Lynn told Jim when he was finished.

"You are welcome. I have a little homework assignment for you to test your learning. Broken links are a problem on most websites. There are contributed modules that check links, but broken links are also logged in Drupal's watchdog logs. Generally, to view the logs, you have to be an administrator, but as Drupal 8 exposes them to Views, why don't you build a view to display *file not found* errors in a block? You can set the block permissions to display only to authenticated users."

"This will be an interesting challenge. Thanks! I'll work on it later this week when I have some time. I need to run and pick up my son now."

"Great, let me know when you're done, and I'll check it out. By the way, this view will only work on your development server as we replaced the watchdog log module with the Syslog module on production to save writing log information into the database. But it is a good exercise and shows one of the new View Types added in Drupal 8."

Showing the Watchdog logs

That weekend, Lynn finally had time for Jim's homework. She decided that a block showing the five most recent errors would be available for everyone who could log in. At the bottom of this block would be a **See more** link to go to a page that showed all the *page not found* errors in a table format.

Adding the Views

Again starting at the Views listing page (**Manage | Structure | Views**), Lynn clicked on the **Add new view** button. She then completed the following fields:

- **View name: Page Not Found Errors**
- **Description**: field checked with text **Display URLs of page not found errors from the Drupal Watchdog log**
- **VIEW SETTINGS Show: Log entries**
- **Sorted by: Newest first**
- **PAGE SETTINGS Create a page**: field checked
- **Page title: Page Not Found Errors**
- **Path: administration/page-not-found-errors**
- **PAGE DISPLAY SETTINGS Display format: Table of fields**
- **Items to display: 25**
- **Use a pager**: field checked
- **Create a menu link**: field unchecked
- **Include an RSS feed**: field unchecked
- **BLOCK SETTINGS Create a block**: field checked
- **Block title: Most Recent Page Not Found Errors**
- **BLOCK DISPLAY SETTINGS Display format: Unformatted list** of **Fields**
- **Items per block: 5**
- **Use a pager**: field unchecked

The form just before Lynn clicked on **Save and edit** looked like this:

Adding a new view for the watchdog error display

The view edit page

At the view edit page, Lynn noticed that there were two displays defined from the previous page. As usual, Jackson was curled up next to the monitor, and Lynn said, somewhat absentmindedly, "Let's see which options would apply to both the block and the page."

The view edit page of the view as created in the previous step looked like this:

The view edit screen for the Page Not Found Errors view as created by Views

"I'm not sure what WID is, but it doesn't look too useful, so I think I'll replace it with the URL of the error." Knowing that in Drupal 6, Views displays an error if there aren't any fields, Lynn decided to add the new field and then delete the WID field.

When she clicked on the **Add field** button next to the **FIELDS** label, the following screen was displayed:

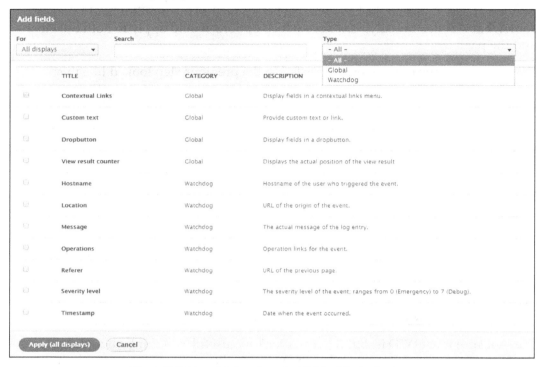

The Add field modal showing select list for filtering by type

Lynn selected the **Watchdog** type filter to limit the options to only fields related to the watchdog logs. Scanning the descriptions, she decided that **URL of the origin of the event** sounded like the URL of the page not found, selected the checkbox next to **Location**, and clicked on the **Apply (all displays)** button.

When you have content with a lot of fields and several relationships, the type and search fields may be the only way of finding the right field to pick. Field names are rarely intuitive, and the description is often your best clue to which one is which. However, all too often, until you see the preview display, you won't know whether you picked the right field. Don't be afraid to try one and see if it works out. If not, delete it and try another one. Still don't see the field you need? Check and make sure you have enough relationships to see the fields. For example, a taxonomy reference in content only has the taxonomy **term ID (TID)**, which is not too useful. To take a look at the actual term, you need the relationship, which will be covered in *Chapter 5, Relationships*.

The next modal had two checkbox options: **Create a label** and **Exclude from display**. Lynn didn't want a label and needed the URL to display, so she left both the options unselected. The fieldsets that followed were options that Lynn didn't know how to use, but she knew from previous experience that they weren't needed for basic views. They were:

- **STYLE SETTINGS**
- **REWRITE RESULTS**
- **NO RESULTS BEHAVIOR**
- **ADMINISTRATIVE TITLE**

"I will dig into these fieldsets later, when I have the time and energy," she said. Then, she clicked on the **Apply (all displays)** button and was back at the view edit screen.

With the new field added, she could delete the WID field added by Views, so she clicked on **Watchdog: WID (WID)** and on the red **Remove** link at the bottom of the modal to the right on the same line as the **Apply (all displays)** button.

"Hmm, these don't look like page not found URLs; they look like administration URLs," she thought. As she scanned the screen, she noticed that there were no filters, so the view was displaying the URLs for every log entry, not just the *page not found* errors. Clicking on the **Add** button next to **FILTER CRITERIA**, she saw a selection screen very much like adding a new field. She selected **Type** and clicked on **Apply (all displays)**, which led to another modal, **Configure filter criterion: Watchdog: Type**, for the criteria to use with type to select which log entries to display. Lynn selected the **is one of** option under **operator** and the **page not found** option under **options**.

Note that the *page not found* option will be listed on this screen only if there are any records for this in the database. If there are no records in the database for pages not found, the only option is **Select all**. Whether this is intentional or a side effect of how this option list is generated isn't clear. However, this means that you need to make sure the options you are looking for are represented in the watchdog table before setting up the filter.

Also, don't be surprised if, as you explore Views, you discover other unusual behavior for certain combinations of fields, options, and confusion as to whether there is data or not.

Lynn could have selected more than one option and Views would display any log entry that had any one of those options as its type (a logical union or an OR selection). For numerical and string fields, there are more options for operators that can allow partial string matches (includes) and ranges of value or greater than / less than. She clicked on the **Apply (all displays)** button and returned to the view edit screen. "That's better."

The last option she changed that applied to both the block and the page was **Access** under **BLOCK SETTINGS** in the center column.

Generally in Views, when you see two option values next to each other, both of which are links (such as the aforementioned **Access** or **Format** and **Show** in the first column), the options available in the second value are determined by the first. Select the first option before you try changing the second, otherwise the options might not make sense (and Views will end up taking you from the first to the second automatically).

Clicking on the **Permissions** link, Lynn changed the option from **permission** to **role**. As the previous setting for the criteria was permissions and not roles, Views immediately went to the criteria modal when the **Apply (all displays)** button was clicked on. Later, she could click on the roles listed to change which roles to allow to view the block or page. She selected **Authenticated user**, which is anyone who is logged in and includes all the other roles by inference, except anonymous, which is a typical visitor. She clicked on the **Apply** button to exit the modal.

You should always have some access criteria selected (never select the **Access: none** option). If your view is misconfigured, you might display information you don't want the average anonymous visitor seeing.

Clicking on the **Save** button to save her work to this point, Lynn asked Jackson, "What do you think, quit for the night or keep working on this view?" Jackson was involved in playing with a spare USB cable that happened to be sitting on Lynn's desk and didn't even look up at Lynn. "Keep working it is. Let's do the block display first as it is the easiest," she said.

"It's pretty close to being ready just as it is, but I think it would be more useful if it included the date and time of the error." She clicked on the **Add** button to the right of the fields label in the first column. In the field selection modal, she selected **Watchdog** in the **Type** filter to limit the fields to those of interest. Scanning the list, she saw **Timestamp** with the description **Date when the event occurred**. Thinking to herself, "I probably will want the same information on the full list," she clicked on the **Apply (all displays)** button.

The next modal that appeared looked similar to the following:

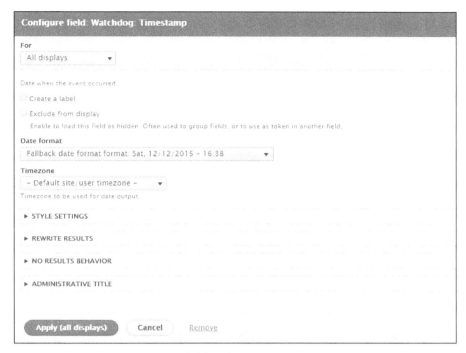

Date field configuration options

Scanning the form, Lynn decided that she didn't need a label on this display. She realized that for the full page display, which was a table, she'd need it; so, she made a note to override it later when she did that display. She selected default medium format, which displays the date and time as *Sat, 12/10/15 – 13:48*. While she wasn't thrilled with military time, she didn't want to go through the process of defining a new date format, which was a several step process in the previous versions of Drupal. "It's an internal administrative display, so this will be okay," she said, more to herself than to Jackson, who was still playing with the cable. The rest of the options were fine for this view, so she clicked on the **Apply (all displays)** button at the bottom.

The preview looked okay, so she clicked on the **Save** button to save her work so far. Moving on to the main page display, she clicked on **Page** at the top of the edit screen. Knowing that she had left the label off the timestamp field, she clicked on this field in the **Fields** section. She selected the **This page (override)** option in the **For** pull-down. Next, she clicked on the checkbox next to **Create a label** and filled in the **Label** field that appeared with **Date and Time of Error**. The rest of the fields could stay the same, so she clicked on the **Apply (this display)** button at the bottom.

Thinking that there should be more displayed on this page, she clicked on the **Add** button next to **Fields**. Scanning the list, she decided that if the **Location** field was the URL of the missing file, then the **Referrer** field must be the URL of the page where the missing file was supposed to be displayed. She set the **For** pull-down option to **This page (override)**, created a label that she called **Page with broken link**, and clicked on the **Apply (this display)** button at the bottom.

"Almost perfect," she said, "But I think I'd rather see the date and time first, then the bad URL, and finally the page with the broken link." Knowing that the **Add** button was actually a pull-down, Lynn selected **Rearrange**, which showed the following modal:

Rearranging fields after dragging the Timestamp field to be first.

Lynn clicked on the **+** drag and drop handle of the **Timestamp** field and dragged it to the first position in the list. Then, she clicked on the **Apply (this display)** button. Looking at the resulting preview, she decided that this was what Jim had asked for. She could see some improvements, such as figuring out a way to limit the list to links from this site only and possibly allowing the user to change the sort order, but these weren't what Jim asked for, and she knew that the view wouldn't survive the trip to production. So, she clicked on **Save**. She then sent the following e-mail:

To: Jim

From: Lynn

Subject: Done

Ok Jim the bad links view is done. It is named Page Not Found Errors (Log entries). The page display is at http://dev.bluedroprealty.com/administration/page-not-found-errors. I even added a block which is on the front page in the left column.

"Good enough, Jackson! Let's get you a nice midnight snack, and it's time for bed." Jackson perked up since he was getting tired of the cable, and they left the room.

Summary

In this chapter, Lynn built a simple table of properties for sale, displaying the address and asking price, number of bedrooms, square footage, and neighborhood. Jim explained the various terms that Views uses to define a view: View Type, display, display type, and Display Contents, going through each option for these terms and the possible uses. Finally, Lynn built a view of bad links, adding both a page and a block display using another table Display Format for the page and an unformatted list Display Format for the block.

In the next chapter, we'll extend the properties list to have better sorting and filtering, including a multilevel sort, and use exposed filters to let site visitors customize the information being displayed, making the site interactive instead of full of static content.

3
Sorting and Filtering

This chapter introduces sorting and filtering. Using Views' default sorting of the last updated date/time and list of all properties wouldn't be too useful for a large real estate agency that may have hundreds of properties, especially if a visitor was looking for a house that has been for sale for quite a while. Sorting lets you specify the order you want your results to be displayed in, and you can also sort within sorts, which is called a multilevel sort. Once we have the properties in a reasonable order, we'll learn how to group the results when there is more than one row with the same value. Next, we will move on to limiting which results are displayed using filtering. The simplest filters are fixed at the time you create a View, such as whether to include unpublished nodes. You can also expose a filter to the user and let them select which results to show.

Changing the sort order

"You know, Jackson, my property list will not be very useful if the only way people can view it is in the order of when we added the properties to the website." Jackson had taken up his usual position next to Lynn's monitor; this time, he brought a toy of his own to play with. "But there is this whole section in the View edit screen labeled **Sort Criteria**, so let's see whether we can figure out a more reasonable way to order this list."

Deleting a sort criteria

Lynn decided to delete the default sort criteria **Content: Authored on**. Thinking that she could delete a sort criteria using the same pull-down that she would use to add a sort criteria, she tried it and was surprised to find only **Add** and **Rearrange** as options. "Hmm, this isn't obvious, is it, Jackson"?

Then, remembering that when she is editing content, there is a **Delete** link at the bottom of the edit screen next to **Save**, she decided to try editing the one sort criteria listed. So, she clicked on the title **Content: Authored on**. The modal that displayed looked similar to the following:

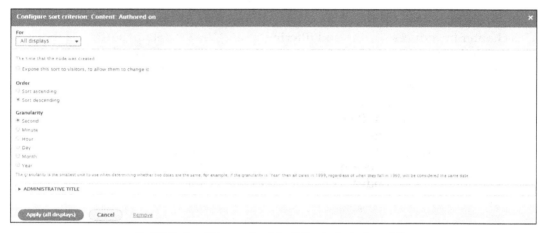

Sort Criteria edit screen for default Content: Authored On

"There it is Jackson, right next to **Apply (all displays)** and **Cancel**, a **Remove** link." So, she clicked on the red **Remove** link and then had an empty sort criteria section. She noticed that the preview got updated and showed a list of property titles. They were in a different order than before, but she didn't see an obvious order. She made a mental note that if she wanted to control the order of a View, it should have at least one sort criteria for any display.

Adding a sort criteria

With the empty sort criteria section, Lynn clicked on **Add** to add a new sort criteria to her view. The modal that resulted looked similar to this:

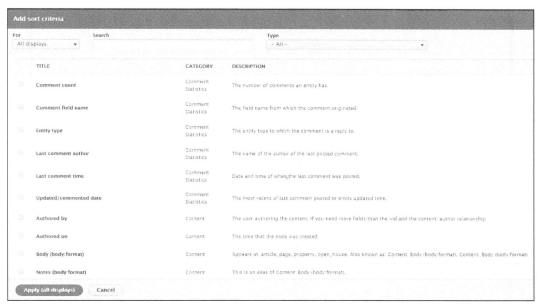

The Add new sort criteria screen

When Lynn looked at the long list of possible sort criteria, she realized that there is a huge number of ways to order a simple table. Looking closer, she noticed that not all the fields listed would make sense given the data she is displaying in this View. The View is of the content of the "property" type, and there are fields shown that are from other content types, users and taxonomies that aren't in this View.

You can add fields from other content types as sort criteria, or even as fields, and Views does its very best to create an SQL query that attempts to join the extra tables to the query for the data you are trying to display. In almost every case, there isn't any relationship to create the SQL join on, so the result is empty for this field. Sorting a group of empty fields for all practical purposes is a "no operation." It does significantly slow down the query, especially on sites with a lot of nodes.

Lynn also noticed that there appeared to be multiple copies of the same field, but when she looked at the description, she realized that they were usually for different content types. She made a mental note to be careful when selecting fields in Views to make sure that the field she was selecting was for the content type she wanted.

It is common to add a sort criteria with a pretty good idea of what the preview data should look like or at least what order it should be in. Sometimes, the preview doesn't look right. So what went wrong? It is possible that you selected the wrong field or that some relationship wasn't defined, so Views didn't get the connection right. If things aren't going the way you expect, try adding the same field to your fields to be output. If you don't see the values you expect, most often, you'll see blank results; then, double check and make sure you have the right field selected. If you have the right field, is it in a related content type and not the primary contact type, such as a realtor's name when doing a view of properties? If so, you will likely need a relationship, covered in *Chapter 5, Relationships*. Adding the field to the fields to be displayed can easily be reversed by removing it when you have the problem you are trying to diagnose resolved.

Lynn decided to start off enhancing her property listing by ordering the listings by address, which in this content type, is the title field. She left the default **Sort ascending order**.

"This is an improvement, but still not the best way to display the listings, I think. Let's try improving this by adding the neighborhood."

Multilevel sorts

Lynn clicked on **Add** and selected the **Property Neighborhood (field_property_ neighborhood)** field, again keeping the default **Sort ascending order**.

"Hmm, this didn't seem to change anything, Jackson. I wonder why." Jackson had been snoozing and looked up quizzically at Lynn.

Multilevel sorts work by sorting on the first sort criteria or key. Then, if there are any values in this resulting list that are the same, the sort will order them by the second sort criteria and so on if there are more than two sort criteria. Having multilevel sorts is a good idea if the content you are sorting has fields that have a limited number of values, such as the neighborhood in Lynn's case. Having a second sort criteria gives order to all the properties within a given neighborhood. Sometimes, but relatively rarely, each of the sort criteria is a little less duplicative than the previous, but still not unique. In these cases, you'd need more than two sort criteria.

Lynn stared at the sort criteria with a frustrated look on her face. Then, it dawned on her what the problem was. When she added the neighborhood after adding the title/address, Views put the sort criteria in the order that she had added them. She thought to herself, I guess this makes sense. Had I planned my sorting out ahead of time, I probably would have added them in the order I was expecting them to work: neighborhood first and then address.

Fortunately for Lynn, when she was looking for how to delete the default sort criteria, she saw the **Rearrange** option in the pull-down that had the **Add** button she had been using. Clicking on the **Rearrange** button, she saw the following display:

Rearranging the sort criteria using Views' drag and drop interface.

Lynn grabbed the drag and drop marker to the left of **Content: Property Neighborhood (asc)**, dragged it over the **Content: Title (asc)** criteria, and clicked on **Apply (all displays)**. The result was exactly what Lynn was expecting. "That's better," she said as she clicked on the **Save** button to save the View.

Grouping

"The neighborhood field is a bit redundant when the View is sorted by neighborhood," Lynn said as she was admiring the updated property list page. "I bet I can make it look better and make more room using the grouping field I saw in the table **Display format** settings."

As of Drupal 8.0.1, grouping in tables fails to add the caption to show the grouping field. In other Display Formats, such as in an unformatted list, if you add a grouping field, each group is preceded by the value of the grouping field as a caption. This is documented in the issue at `https://www.drupal.org/node/2302319`. A patch, `missing_caption_if-2302319-57.patch`, appears to resolve the problem. Most likely, by the time this book comes out, the patch will be committed and released, but check the issue status if you don't see a caption.

Lynn clicked on **Settings** next to **Table** in the **Format** section of the View edit screen. In the settings modal, she selected **Neighborhood** in the **Grouping Field Nr. 1** select pull-down. She clicked on **Apply**, looked at the preview for the view, and saw the following:

A preview of the view with the grouping field selected for Neighborhood

"That's better, but now I need to get rid of Neighborhood on each line." Lynn clicked on the **Content: Property Neighborhood (Neighborhood)** field to check the settings for this field. She selected the box next to **Exclude from display**, which looked like the right solution, especially as the description for this setting was **Enable to load this field as hidden. Often used to group fields, or to use as token in another field**. Remembering that she had other displays, specifically the RSS feed, that might need the field, she changed the **For** to **This page (override)** and clicked on **Apply (this display)**.

The resulting preview looked similar to the following:

A preview of the view with the grouping field and the hidden Neighborhood field

Lynn clicked on **Save** to save the results of her efforts and said, "This works for me, Jackson. What do you say, let's take a break?" Jackson was in favor of that idea and came over to get a tummy rub.

Exposed sort fields

When Lynn got back to work, she wondered what the **Expose this sort to visitors, to allow them to change it** option would be useful for. Deciding to take a look, she edited the **Content: Property Neighborhood** sort field by clicking on it, and in the settings modal, she enabled the option for the **Neighborhood** field, changed the label to read just **Neighborhood**, and clicked on **Apply (this display)**. In the preview, she saw two pull-down select lists appear in the **Exposed Filters** section. One pull-down, **Sort by**, only had one option: **Neighborhood**. "That's odd", thought Lynn. The other pull-down, **Order**, had two options: **Asc** and **Desc**. "That's more what I was expecting." Selecting **Desc** caused the View to be displayed sorted in a descending order. "This could be useful to let people see the end of a long table quickly." However, the select with one option bothered Lynn. Deciding to take the experiment a little further, she enabled the **Expose this sort to visitors, to allow them to change it** option for her other sort criteria, **Title**. Now, the preview showed two options: **Title** and **Neighborhood**. The preview select options looked similar to this:

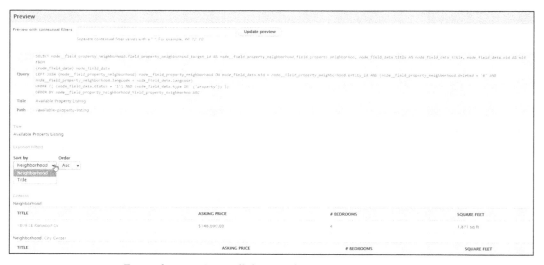

Exposed sort options pull-down with two sort criteria exposed

When she selected **Title**, the preview was ordered by address instead of **Neighborhood**. "That's clever. It would let a site builder give the option of how to sort a list for the visitor." She decided to save this idea for another display. "If I wanted to let visitors sort this table, I think using the sortable column listing would make more sense, plus I'd have to put the hidden field back and not do the grouping I have now." Lynn clicked on **Cancel** to keep the view the way she had it before the experiment.

Don't be afraid to try things. There are a lot of options in Views, more than a reasonable-length book could cover in detail. When you see an option that doesn't seem clear or might be useful, try it. You will find all sorts of powerful settings you can use.

Alternatively, you can duplicate (clone in the previous versions) an entire view and either experiment on the copy or use the copy as a backup in case you do something to the original View that you can't undo.

Filtering results

Lynn got a call from Jim, who got her e-mail that she had built the *page not found* View and noticed that she had been building other views on the development site. "Hi Lynn, I wanted to call and let you know that you went above and beyond what I asked for with your View to display *page not found* errors. Did you have any questions building this view?"

Lynn answered, "Hi Jim. Actually, building the *page not found* errors was pretty straightforward. I even saw how to use some of the great information you gave me over coffee to add another block display. Thanks for that session; it was really helpful."

"You're welcome. I see that you have been working on the *Property Listing* page View. Any questions so far?"

"Good timing. I was just wondering how to build a View to show unpublished properties or open houses so that Amanda and I can quickly review them and get them published. I was thinking of basing the View off the general Drupal content maintenance View. But I'm not really sure how to pick just the unpublished properties and open houses. Any hints?"

"Sure, I'll give you a hint and let you discover how to apply the hint yourself. This way, you'll learn more about how Views does things. Take a close look at the **Filter Criteria** section of your View edit screen. Enough of a hint?"

"I had a feeling that you would make me work for the answer, but I appreciate that. I'll take your hint and see how it goes. If I have a problem, can I call you?"

"Sure", replied Jim.

"Great, I'll either call or send you an e-mail if I figure it out." With that, Lynn hung up the phone and went to work discovering how Views does filtering.

The "To Be Published" View for administrators

Lynn was thinking about the publishing workflow she wanted for properties and open houses. She didn't want anyone to be able to add a property or open house and have it just appear on the website. She also didn't want to wait for a complex module such as Workbench Moderation to be ported to Drupal 8. She had talked over her options with Jim, and he had suggested she set the Property and Open House content types to default to *unpublished* and not give real estate salespeople the **Manage content** permission so that they couldn't change the defaults in the content creation or editing screens. Then, she and her office manager, Amanda, would have the ability to change the status of the new content to *published* to have it appear on the site to visitors.

"Okay, Jackson, let's see whether we can make a View show unpublished content to make it easier for Amanda and me to find and see unpublished content on the site." Lynn knew that she wanted something a lot like the built-in **Content** view that Drupal uses to manage content, so she duplicated the View as a starting point and called it "To Be Published".

At the View edit screen, she started off focused on the **Filter Criteria** section of the View as that's the part of the View she most wanted to change. She was surprised that there were so many criteria already defined and decided to look at each one to see what it did:

- **Content: Published status or admin user**: This predefined filter is described as **Filters out unpublished content if the current user cannot view it**. It looks at the user's permissions, and if they have permission to see the content being displayed, they will see it in this View. This option deals with differing permissions that can be assigned to various site builder-created roles.

- **Content: Publishing status (grouped)**: This exposed filter allows users to select between published and unpublished using a group filter option, defaulting to both.

- **Content: Type (exposed)**: This exposed filter allows user to select which content type to view, defaulting to all.

- **Content: Title (exposed)**: This exposed filter matches the string with any part of a content title to select what is displayed.

- **Content: Translation language (exposed)**: This predefined exposed filter allows the translation language to be used to select what content is displayed. Options include **Select all**, **Site's default language (English)**, **Interface text language selected for page**, **Content language selected for page**, **English**, **Not specified**, and **Not applicable**.

Lynn decided to delete the translation language filter, and did so by selecting it and clicking on **Remove**. For the publishing status, she decided to delete the existing grouped exposed filter and replace it with a simpler, fixed, not published status filter. So, she also deleted the publishing status filter. She did the same for the first published status or admin user.

Filtering by node status

Having deleted most of the existing filters for the *To Be Published* view, Lynn started adding the filters she thought she needed. First was a "filter by node" status equal to not published. She clicked on the **Add** button for **Filter Criteria** and in the field selection modal, typed publish, and selected **Publishing status**, being careful to pick the one in the **Content** category and not the one in the **Content revision** category.

If your filter isn't working in preview the way you expect, double check that you added the correct field. It is easy to mistakenly select the wrong one, such as the two **Publishing status** fields in this example. When in doubt, only use fields that are related to your content type, taxonomy, and so on. You can limit the fields by the category of the type of the View you are building. If you defined relationship(s) or are using one of the system fields, then additional fields will make sense and produce results. Again, if you don't see what you expect, double check that you are using the right field.

On the **Configure filter criterion: Content: Publishing status** modal, Lynn selected the **Is equal to** operator and **Published status No**. She could have selected **Not equal to** and **Published status Yes** as equivalent. She clicked on the **Apply (all displays)** button to save the result.

Beware of creating views that can display content you don't intend to be seen by all visitors, such as the View that shows unpublished content but is accessible to anyone with the View published content permission, which includes anonymous visitors to the site. Either set the View access in the **Page settings** section or include a permissions filter, such as **Content: Published status or admin user**.

Lynn remembered that Jim had mentioned being careful with views that displayed unpublished content to make sure only the correct people could see them. So, she headed to the **Page settings** section to make sure she had the correct **Access** settings. She clicked on **Permission** and selected **Role**, then on the next modal, she selected the **Administrator** and **Office Manager** roles that would take care of herself and Amanda.

While she was updating the **Access** settings, she updated the path to admin/content/to-be-published. She also changed the **Menu** setting to a **Menu** tab with the **Normal** menu entry title of **To Be Published** and the **Parent** menu item to **--Administration** in the **Administration** menu. When she clicked on **Save** to save her changes to the View, she checked the content menu to see whether the new tab appeared. It hadn't, which confused her; the settings were the same as the files View. Then, she tried clearing caches and reloading the page, and sure enough, the new tab appeared.

A lot of Drupal is cached for performance reasons. If you don't see a change you are pretty sure should be there, try clearing the caches (**Configuration** | **Development** | **Performance**). If this doesn't work for a View, try clearing the view's caches (through the **Structure** | **Views** | **Settings** tab | **Advanced** subtab).

Filtering by content type – compound filters

Lynn only wanted to show the Property and Open House content types in this specialized administrative View. To add the Property content type filter, she clicked on the **Add** button for **Filter Criteria** and in the field selection modal, typed type and selected **Type** in the **Content** category. In the selection modal that followed, Lynn saw that she could check both the Property and Open House content types, and the filter would take care of selecting either type to include in the View. However, Lynn was curious about filter groups, which she had seen when she rearranged the filters on her property listing View. She had asked Jim about filter groups and remembered what he had said about how filters work in general.

"Filters are a way of selecting information when Views creates a query. They are a way to take a very large list of content, for example, and create a manageable list. Most of the time, each and every filter has to be true for the particular piece of information to be selected. However, sometimes, you will want more complex selections. Views can do this with filter groups. Remember that the default filter group is all AND selections. However, if you want to allow an either/or of two selections, you can do this with a filter group. Create both the filters from which you want to choose either/or. Then, you can add the filter group, drag your two filters into this group, and change the filter group operation from AND to OR. Note that when you add a filter group, yet another operation is created and defaults to AND. This operation is how the results of the filter group you are creating should be interpreted in relation to the other filters."

Lynn decided that as this was a great opportunity to figure out how filter groups work, she'd use a filter group instead of the two options in the **Type** filter, even though it was a bit of overkill. So, she created the first **Type** filter with just **Property** and added a second **Type** filter with just **Open House**.

With the two filters created, Lynn used the **And/or Rearrange** button to display the rearrange modal. In this modal, under the **For All Displays** selector, is a link labeled **Create new filter group**. She clicked on this link and saw the following screen:

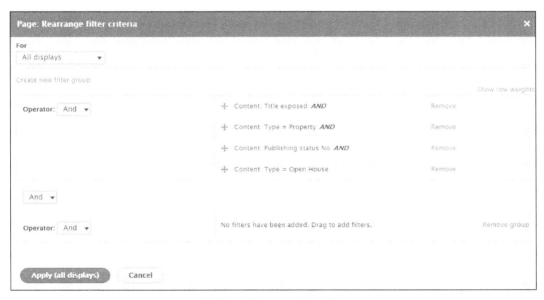

Adding a filter group to a View

Lynn set the operator for the new filter group to **OR** and dragged the two **Content Type** filters below the line that showed **No filters have been selected. Drag to add filters**. The resulting configuration modal looked similar to the following:

After dragging the filters into the new group

Finally, Lynn clicked on **Apply (all displays)**, and the resulting View **Filter Criteria** section looked similar to the following:

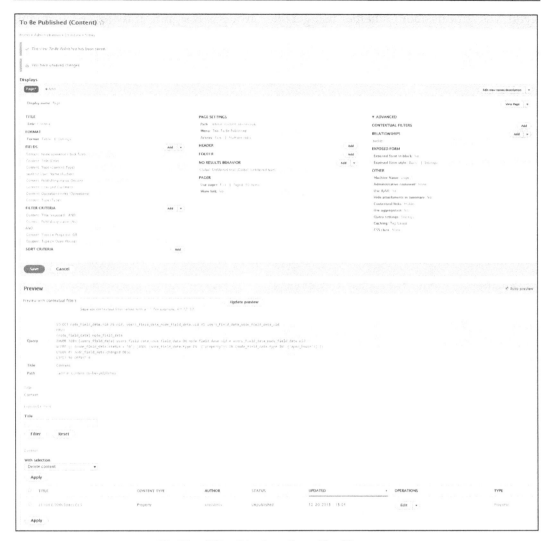

The View Filter Criteria section with a filter group

Lynn was curious about whether using a filter group was significantly less performant than a single filter that she could have used. So, she saved the SQL queries displayed by the two options and sent them to Jim. His response was encouraging:

To: Lynn

From: Jim

Subject: Filter SQL

From what I can see, both queries are pretty much the same except for the WHERE clause, which isn't surprising since that is what the filter criteria affects. Using the single filter with an either-or results in a WHERE clause as follows:

```
WHERE (( (node_field_data.type IN  ('open_house', 'property')) AND
(node_field_data.status = '0') ))
```

While the grouped filter results in a WHERE clause as follows:

```
WHERE (( (node_field_data.status = '0') )AND( (node_field_data.type IN
('property')) OR (node_field_data.type IN  ('open_house')) ))
```

Since both WHERE clauses are doing tests on the same fields, just with different logic, the calls to the database are about the same and I would not expect to see an appreciable difference in execution time.

Thanks for sending this over, I learned something new today!

Jim

Lynn finished the view by changing the **Content: Node operations bulk form** field to only allow two options: publish content and unpublish content. She clicked on **Save** to save the resulting View.

Filtering by field value

Lynn has been watching a show on the FYI cable channel called "Tiny House Nation" after customers started coming in and asking for tiny houses. It is an interesting show, and the movement to live in less than 500 square feet seems to be gaining popularity. While Blue Springs hasn't actually developed a tiny house market, Lynn decided that she can capitalize on the movement and the TV show by having a page that lists any properties less than 500 square feet.

Lynn decided that this could be done with the current property listing View by adding an additional filter for property size. Going to the Views listing page, she edited the *Available Property Listing* View. As this listing was going to be the same as a regular property listing with the additional filter, she felt that it made sense to just create another page display for tiny houses. So, she clicked on the **+Add** button, which was actually a pull-down and selected **Page** to create a new page display. She changed **Display Name** from **Page 2** to **Tiny Houses**. She also set the path for the page to `tiny-houses`. Then, she gave the page a menu link on the navigation menu.

Along with the housekeeping edits to the display, Lynn added the filter for less than 500 square feet. She clicked on the **Add** button next to **Filter Criteria**. Typing `square` into the search field, she selected the only option, **Property Square Footage (field_property_square_footage)**. Lynn didn't want to add the filter to all displays, just this one; so, when she saw the button read **Apply (all displays)**, it reminded her to change the **For** field at the top to **This page (override)**. The blue button changed to read **Apply (this display)**, so Lynn clicked on it.

On the next modal, she selected **Is less than or equal to** under **Operator** and typed `500` into the **Value** field. She clicked on the **Apply (this display)** button and looked at the resulting preview. There was one property that was barely less than 500 square feet at 499 square feet. However, she could take advantage of the Tiny House publicity. When she launched the new site, she made a note to post the URL of the page onto Tiny House's Facebook page.

Exposed filters – giving power to your visitors

Inspired by the Tiny House page, Lynn thought to herself "I wonder whether I can let visitors select the property listings that meet certain criteria and get a customized list." Remembering the experience she had while experimenting with the exposed sort and that she had noticed the **Expose this filter to visitors, to allow them to change it** option, she decided to make a page that included exposed filters for the number of bedrooms, square footage, price range, and neighborhood.

Lynn decided to make this selectable View another display in case she wanted to have the unfiltered option somewhere, so she clicked on the **+Add** button on the property listing View page and selected **Page**. She changed the display name from **Page 3** to **Selectable Page** so that she could recognize it easier. She decided that the page title **Available Property Listing** still applied, so she didn't change it.

She clicked on **Add** to add a new filter criteria and typed Square into the search box on the available fields modal. She selected **Property Square Footage (field_property_square_footage)**, selected **This page (override)**, and clicked on **Apply (this display)**. On the next modal, she selected the **Expose this filter to visitors, to allow them to change it** option, and the modal changed to look similar to the following:

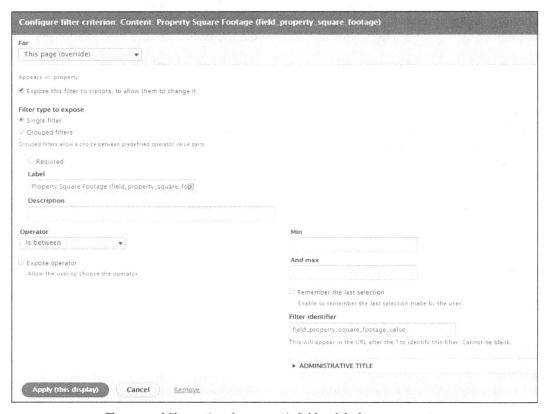

The exposed filter options for a numeric field and the between operator.

Lynn changed the label to **Square Footage** and selected the **Remember the last selection** option, which displayed the roles that should be allowed to remember the last selection. Lynn selected both **Anonymous** and **Authenticated**, which covers both visitors and anyone who can log in. She clicked on **Apply (this display)**.

Similar to the table caption issue, as of Drupal 8.0.1, selecting a numeric exposed filter with a range (between) option doesn't output the label, which makes the view confusing. This is a known issue documented at `https://www.drupal.org/node/2480719`. This was fixed in 8.0.2 in January. The point of this is that when you find something that doesn't work as it should, you can search the *drupal.org/project/drupal* issue queue, and if you can't find an issue that relates to what you are seeing/not seeing (look at all issues, including ones that are closed), then *you should file an issue about your problem*. The community needs this feedback to know what problems need fixing.

She repeated the same steps for **Property Asking Price (field_property_asking_price)**, changing the label to **Asking Price**.

She did it one more time for **Property Number Bedrooms (field_property_number_bedrooms)**, changing the label to **# Bedrooms**.

For the last filter, neighborhood, she added a filter for **Property Neighborhood (field_property_neighborhood)**. As this field is actually a taxonomy reference, the options were considerably different and are presented on two modal screens. The first modal screen looks similar to the following:

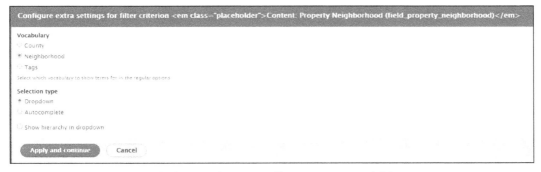

The first set of options to filter on a taxonomy field

Lynn selected the **Neighborhood** vocabulary and decided that a drop-down selection type would let visitors pick from a list rather than know what neighborhoods were defined for the Blue Drop website. She clicked on **Apply and continue** and was presented with a second, more complex modal with lots of options, which looked similar to the following:

The second set of options to filter on taxonomy with the options Lynn selected

Exposed filter options

The first option, **Expose this filter to visitors, to allow them to change it**, was obvious, and she checked it. For the second option, **Filter type to expose**, she had some idea what grouped filters were based on looking at the content view when she modified it, so she selected **Single filter**. Selecting **Single filter** exposed the terms and other options without any limitations. This seemed to make sense in this case because she just wanted to allow people to pick one or more neighborhoods.

> Had she wanted to, she could have selected **Grouped filters**, which allow the visitor a choice between operators and value pairs that the site builder preselected. In the content view, Drupal uses a grouped filter to select between published and not published, taking a Boolean value of TRUE or FALSE and changing it to more recognizable terms, published and unpublished. A more complex example would be of bathrooms, where the options might be **1**, defined as less than or equal to 1.5 (most people don't consider a half bathroom to be a selection); **2**, defined as 2 to 2.5; **3**, defined as 3 to 3.5; and **More than 3**, defined as greater than or equal to 4 (I know the last definition is a bit counterintuitive). In this example, both the operator (less than, between or greater than, or equal) and the values are different, yet the visitor is given a simple four-way selection pull-down.

Lynn changed the label to **Neighborhood** and set the operator to **Is one of**, which would let a visitor select any of the terms from the neighborhood taxonomy. As it is very possible that a visitor would be interested in houses from more than one neighborhood, she selected **Allow multiple selections**. As with the other exposed filters, she selected **Remember the last selection** and made the option available to both anonymous and authenticated users. She left **Display error message** enabled, although she made a note to ask Jim about it later as she had no idea what the option was for. Finally, she selected **Reduce duplicates**. By selecting the option, even though each neighborhood might show up multiple times, it would only result in one row of the results displaying.

When she had all the options for the neighborhood taxonomy exposed filter selected, Lynn clicked on **Apply (this display)** to save the filter for just this display, leaving the general list, tiny house list, and RSS feeds unchanged.

While the selections were formatted funnily and could be confusing, they worked as Lynn expected them to. She knew that one of Jim's developers could theme the exposed filters to put one filter per line and draw a box around the pair of options, so at this point, just the functionality was important to her. Making the site more usable would be part of the theming just before site launch.

Lynn clicked on **Save** to save the results of her exposed filter display and took a look at the page she had created with this display. It looked similar to the following:

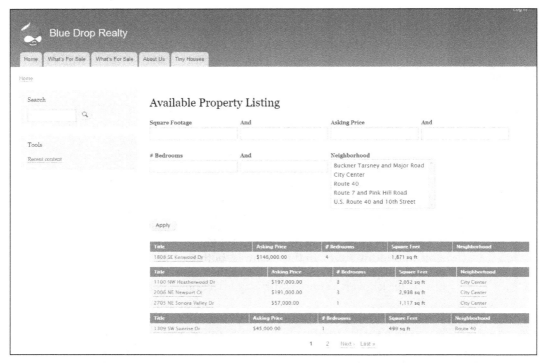

A page showing available property listing with exposed filters to select what is displayed

"Jackson, you have been very patient with me during this marathon. How about we get you a treat, and we both watch a movie with the family?" Lynn gave Jackson a quick pet before getting up and turning off the lights. Jackson decided it was time to leave the room with her rather than sit in the dark alone.

Summary

Drupal's default sorting isn't very useful. We showed how to set up single-level and multilevel sorting, then added exposed sorts. Using an exposed sort gives visitors flexibility in how they view the content not contained in tables, which can use the built-in sortable columns options. From order, we covered filtering. Filtering lets a View builder control what information should be displayed, selecting a subset of the query-generated extracts from the database. For those who know SQL, this is the WHERE clause in most SQL queries. Exposed filters again give the visitor more control of how and what is displayed—in our example, limiting property listings by size (bedrooms), cost, and/or neighborhood.

In the next chapter, we'll extend the exposed filter concept to the ways by which Drupal sites can pass the filter criteria via the URL as well as use information from the page being displayed to control the information displayed in a block. These are called contextual filters and are a powerful addition to your Views repertoire. Even though they are administered in the **Advanced** column of the View edit screen, they are a natural extension of the filters you created in this chapter. Contextual filters use the URL to pass the selection criteria to the filter. Contextual filters also have powerful default value settings that can be used to take context that isn't obvious, such as who is logged in, to filter the output. Using these default filters, we can pass the parameters to a block, which may not be intuitively obvious.

4
Contextual Filters

In the last chapter, sorting and filtering was explained. Sorting lets site builders specify what order their data lists should be in. Filtering lets site builders select just a portion of a large list, such as the Tiny House page that selects properties of less than 500 square feet from the total list of available properties. Exposed filters allow visitors to select the values or ranges of values that are most interesting to them, making the lists of data more interactive and useful.

Filters require the site builder to select the values or expose the filter to allow the visitor to select the values. As a result, it is common to see a single view with a dozen displays, each with a filter or two set to specific values, such as a neighborhood. There is a better way that allows Drupal to take a value from the URL or use information gathered from what page is displayed to filter results. This capability is called contextual filtering. Even though contextual filters are in the third, **Advanced** column, they are really just another kind of filter, so we'll cover them now, right after the other Views filter options. Most of the concepts are the same; just the way the criteria is passed is unique.

Contextual filters are filters in a different place

Lynn picked up the phone and dialed Jim. When he answered, she said "Jim, do you have time for a couple of quick questions?"

"Sure, what can I help you with?"

"Great. When I was adding my improvements to the available property listing with exposed filters, on the taxonomy filter for neighborhoods, there was an option, **Display error message**. Do you have any idea of what this option does? It's not a big deal; I left it enabled, and it doesn't seem to affect how the view is working, but I am curious about it."

Jim replied, "I have no clue. Let me ask the developers here if they know, or they can find out. Do you have any questions I would know the answer to?"

"Ok, let's move on to one I remember you telling me before. On our current site, I did a series of view pages that showed the listings for a given neighborhood. I built it using a filter for the neighborhood and by creating a new view display for each neighborhood. I remember you saying that there was a way of using contextual filters, but at the time, I didn't have the time or inclination to figure out what you meant. I see filters, and I understand how to make them exposed, but how do I make them contextual?"

"This is a bit confusing," Jim replied. "Contextual filters work a whole lot like a regular filter or exposed filter, but they get the value to filter by from the URL, so while you'd expect that they'd be defined in the filter section of the view, they aren't. They are actually part of the third column of the view edit screen in the fieldset labeled **Advanced**. If you didn't set the Views setting to always show the **Advanced** display settings, you could very easily overlook them."

Lynn confessed, "I've got my settings the way you recommended, but to be honest, I've been ignoring this column as it was labeled **Advanced**, and I figure I'm not advanced enough to try it yet."

"It's just a label, don't let that keep you from the neat stuff it can do. You'll find that using contextual filters is a whole lot like using regular filters. If you want, we can meet up, and I can show them to you, but I have a feeling that you will understand them if you take a look with the possible exception of how Drupal does default values, which can be very powerful and a bit mysterious."

"That's a really nice offer, Jim, but I've taken up enough of your time. Let's see how I do on my own. I will build an image map that links to each neighborhood's list of available properties. Yes, I know that image maps aren't a good idea in this age of mobile phones, but I am experimenting for now. We can discuss an alternative if the visitor is on a mobile device later, when we're closer to launching the site. I'll call if I get stuck."

"Okay, good luck, and let me know when you have something to look at."

Adding an image map linked to neighborhood listings

Lynn took the image of the neighborhood map for Blue Ridge and uploaded it to a website called **Easy Imagemap Generator**, found via Google, that let Lynn create the HTML she needed for the image map after she traced the rough outlines of the various neighborhoods. As there were neighborhoods that she hadn't set up, for now, she just used the closest neighborhood with the expectation of coming back later and cleaning it up if she decided to keep the image map when the site launched. She took the HTML code and created an article page, using it to upload the image, and then pasted the generated HTML code into the body after setting the format to **Full HTML**.

As this new set of pages is basically the same view as the one with exposed filters she had just finished, she decided that she could just duplicate the display she'd created for the exposed filters and replace the exposed neighborhood filter with an equivalent contextual filter. Lynn went to the Views listing page (**Manage | Structure | Views**) and clicked on **Edit** to change the *Available Property Listing* view. Instead of clicking on **+Add** to add a new display, which would have inherited the master or default display's settings, she decided to duplicate the Selectable Page. She clicked on the button labeled **Selectable Page** in the drop-down menu to the right below the grey **Displays** bar. The screen with the pull-down looked similar to this:

Duplicating a display instead of adding a new display and the Options pull-down menu shown

Lynn selected **Duplicate Selectable Page**, which generated a new display. She clicked on **Display name** of **Duplicate of Selectable Page** and changed the name to **Neighborhood Page**. She changed the URL for the page to available-property-list-by-neighborhood, clicked on **Content: Property Neighborhood** under **Filter Criteria**, and clicked on the red **Remove** link to delete the exposed filter of neighborhood.

Adding a contextual filter

Then, with the **Advanced** fieldset at the top of the third column expanded, she clicked on the **Add** button next to **Contextual Filters**. The resulting field selection modal looked just like the **Filter Criteria** selection modal, so she entered neighborhood into the search field and selected **Content: Property Neighborhood (field_property_neighborhood)**.

The next modal looked a bit different from the **Filter Criteria** options she was expecting. It looked similar to the following:

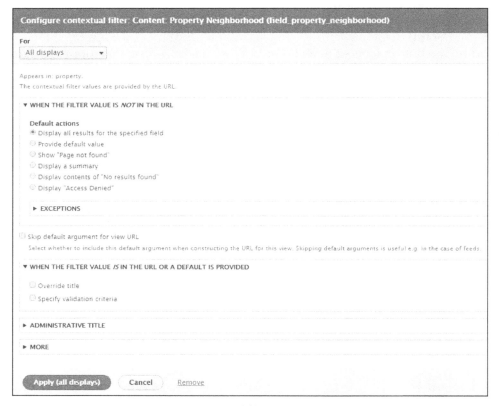

Contextual filter options

"As I will control the links to this page, I probably don't need to deal with what to do if there isn't a value in the URL, so I'll keep the default setting for **WHEN THE FILTER VALUE IS NOT IN THE URL**. But I do want to change the title of the page to show which neighborhood I'm displaying." Lynn realized that she was talking to herself; Jackson had gotten up and wandered off while she was editing the display.

She selected the **Override title** option, and a text field appeared. The description for the field said **You may use Twig syntax in this field**. Lynn knew about using tokens from her previous version of Drupal, so she figured that this was just a change in terminology. Remembering that the key to the tokens was in a collapsed fieldset labeled **Replacement patterns**, she clicked on the heading and read the text that was displayed. She noticed that the tokens that were enclosed in square brackets [ ] before were now enclosed in pairs of curly brackets {{ }}, but otherwise, it looked about the same. She copied the first one and pasted it after **Available Property Listings for** to make the **Available Property Listings for {{arguments. field_property_neighborhood_target_id}}** field. She clicked on **Apply (this display)** and returned to the view edit screen.

When she looked at the preview section, there wasn't anything showing. This had Lynn puzzled for a couple of minutes until she reread the prompt next to an empty text field that said, **Preview with contextual filters**. She typed in `City Center` and clicked on **Update preview**, yet nothing showed. She was just about to call Jim for help when she remembered that the neighborhood field was an entity reference. Also, she remembered that Drupal doesn't store the value(s) in the field but stores the index of the values instead. In the exposed filter selection option, this was hidden from the site builder because Views automatically converted the indexes into the taxonomy term names. However, for a contextual filter designed to be used by the site, the index makes more sense (and saves some SQL join statements).

"How do I find the index for a taxonomy term?" Lynn thought to herself. Then, she remembered that the taxonomy term ID showed in the URL when you edited the term. So, she went to the taxonomy listing page (**Manage | Structure | Taxonomy**) and clicked on **List Terms** for the **Neighborhood** vocabulary. She realized that she didn't need to actually edit each term to find its ID; she could just hover over the **Edit** button for each term and look at the URL displayed. For City Center, the URL was `/taxonomy/term/6/edit`. She built herself a cheat sheet that read:

Buckner Tarsney and Major Road	11
City Center	6
Route 40	16
Route 7 and Pink Hill Road	26
U.S. Route 40 and 10th Street	21

Lynn typed the number 6 in the **Preview with contextual filters** text field and clicked on **Update preview**. This time, the table of listings for City Center appeared along with the remaining exposed filters for square footage, number of bedrooms, and asking price. The only thing that didn't look right was the title for the page, which read **Available Property Listings for 6**. Lynn thought it might be for the same reason that she had to use the index instead of the name and made a note to ask Jim about this when she talked to him next time. As it was getting late, Lynn clicked on **Save** to save the resulting edits to her available listings view. The resulting view looked similar to the following:

The View edit screen for the Neighborhood page display

Finishing the image map

Lynn built the image map article page and pasted the generated HTML from the Easy Imagemap Generator website into the body field, substituting the numbers from her cheat sheet in the various URLs. When she clicked on **Save and publish**, the image map was there, without any adornment that she'd need if she kept it when the site went live, but functioning enough to show that she had figured out how to pass the neighborhood taxonomy term ID via the URL. Satisfied with the progress so far, Lynn went off to join the family in watching TV.

Using default values to "create" options

The next day, feeling refreshed, Lynn decided to tackle the contextual filters default value options. "I think it would be nice to have a list of the properties waiting to be published, or listed as we say, displayed on the user page after they log into the site. As the only users who log in are real estate salespeople who enter the listings but have to wait for my office manager or myself to approve of them, showing the listings still waiting will let them follow up with us if we somehow forget."

Jackson had deemed it sufficiently boring in the house that he was willing to curl up next to Lynn's monitor in his usual spot. Lynn reached up and gave him a quick scratch.

"The simplest solution would be to create a block and have it displayed only on the user's page. This much I know how to do with a standard view and the usual block visibility settings. However, if I want to use a single view display and pass the user ID or username to it as a filter, how does that work? There's no URL for a block to pass a contextual filter value with."

Lynn thought about it a bit while scratching Jackson. "I'll bet the solution is hiding in those default value settings." Jackson purred. He didn't have a clue of what Lynn was talking about but was willing to be scratched no matter what she said.

Lynn originally thought that she could add a block display to the unpublished properties view she had built by adapting the content view that is built into Drupal 8. After creating a new display, she started to delete the extra fields. After she deleted about half the fields taking care not to accidentally select the **Apply (all displays)** option, she realized that a better solution would be to simply create a new view. Fortunately, she hadn't saved her work by the time she came to this realization, so she was able to discard all her changes by simply clicking on **Cancel** instead of **Save**.

From time to time, you will start developing a view and realize that the approach you are taking isn't the best approach. As long as you haven't saved your changes, clicking on **Cancel** will let you try a different approach. If you are really concerned about having a backup option, export your configuration (this is Drupal 8, after all), and you can always reimport it later.

Adding a block view for unpublished properties

Back at the Views listing page, Lynn clicked on **Add new view**, named the new view **Unpublished properties per realtor**, and selected **Show Content of type Property sorted by Newest first**. She selected the **Create a block** option and left the block name as the default. For the block display settings, she selected **Unformatted list of titles (linked)** and **5 Items per block** and clicked on **Save and edit**.

At the view edit screen, she clicked on the default **Block name** and changed it to **Unpublished properties per realtor**. In the same **Block Settings** section, she changed the **Access** option from **Permission** to **Role** and selected the **Administrator, Office Administrator**, and **Real Estate Salesperson** roles. This made the block easy to find on the blocks administration page and made the block so that it would only be displayed for the salespeople, Lynn, and Amanda, her office manager.

Drupal automatically adds a filter criteria for the publishing status equal to published, which is what the user would want for most views. In this case, Lynn wants to specifically show unpublished property listings, so she clicked on the **Publishing status** filter, changed the criteria from **Published status Yes** to **No**, and then clicked on **Apply (all displays)**.

Having set up the basic display and selection criteria and limited the block display to the appropriate roles, Lynn was ready to tackle the contextual filter. She clicked on **Add** next to **Contextual filters** and selected the **Content: Authored by** field to filter by.

Default filter value options

"Okay, Jackson, this was the easy part. Let's see whether we can get *select by the current user* set up as a parameter to this contextual filter." Jackson didn't respond. From the clue from Jim, Lynn decided that the **WHEN THE FILTER VALUE IS NOT AVAILABLE** fieldset was the key to passing the information to the view. "Obviously, the Drupal default of **Display all results for the specified field** isn't a reasonable option, neither are most of the options; the one that looks the most promising is the **Provide default value** option." When she clicked on this option, several options appeared, including a select list for the type of default value. This pull-down showed several options that looked similar to this:

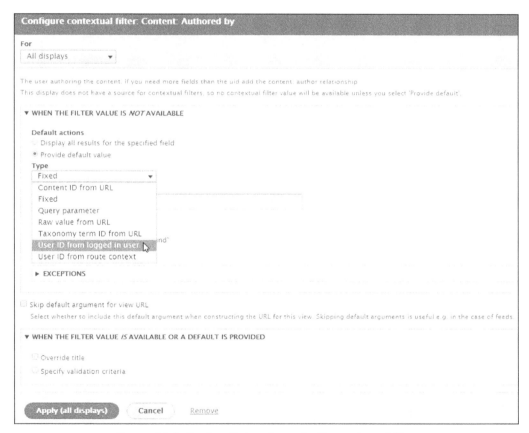

Types of default values that can be used with a contextual filter

Scanning the list of options, Lynn decided the one that made sense in selecting only the properties of the salesperson who was logged in was **User ID from logged in user**, so she selected it and clicked on **Apply (all displays)**. The preview showed the one sample she had edited to have her as the author.

Finishing up the view and testing

Before saving the view, she added a **Global: Text area (Global: Text area)** field to display **You have no properties waiting to be listed** if there are no results for this user, so that salespeople without any listings waiting to be published wouldn't be confused by the block title without a result. She clicked on **Save** for the view and switched to the blocks configuration page (**Manage | Structure | Block layout**). Adding the block in this view just created the content region, and she changed the visibility to only show the block on certain pages with the URL pattern /user/*, which limits the block to user pages. Going to her user page at /user/6, she saw what she wanted, which looked similar to the following:

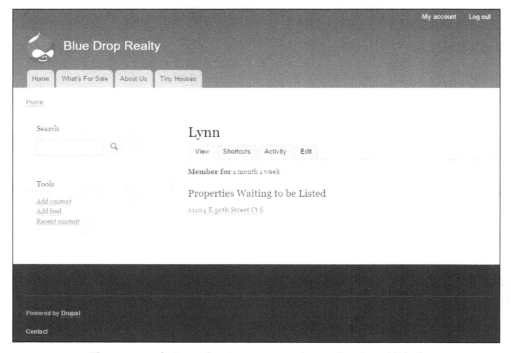

The user page for Lynn showing a property that needs to be published

When she logged into the site using another browser as Sam, one of the salespeople she used as a test user on this site, his user page showed the block title with **You have no properties waiting to be listed** because she hadn't created any unpublished properties with this user as the author. She changed a property using the browser she was logged into so that it was unpublished and had Sam's user ID as the author. She then switched back again, and the block showed one property as needing to be published. Satisfied with her work so far, Lynn picked up the phone and dialed Jim again.

"Hi Jim, I got a view that generates a block on the user page when they log in that shows any properties they created that haven't been published, but I see a lot of other options for contextual filters that aren't really clear to me. I've decided that it might be useful for you to go over them for me."

"Congratulations on getting this much done! Views does have a lot of options for contextual filters, and they can seem overwhelming. How about having coffee at our usual place tomorrow morning before work and I can quickly brief you on what you have seen?"

Contextual filter options explained

They agreed to get together, and the next morning, with cups of coffee in hand, they sat down at a table. Jim started right in using his computer to show the screen as he talked. He pulled up a view and added a contextual filter on the neighborhood just to show the options screen, which is shown here:

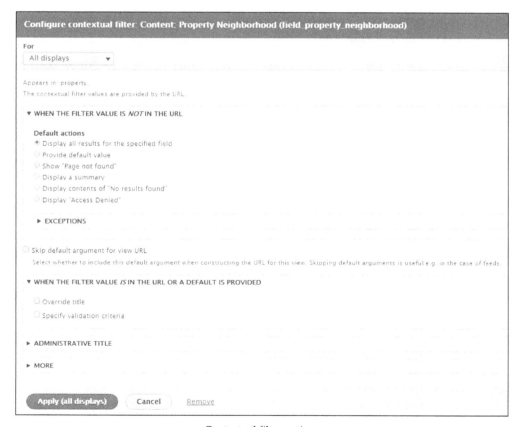

Contextual filter options

Basically, the contextual filter options are broken down into three sections:

- What the filter should do if there isn't a value in the URL
- What the filter should do if there is, and thus includes any default from the first section
- Some other options that are independent of how the value gets set

Options for no value

Looking at the option for what to do when you don't have a value, most of them are pretty obvious. You can choose among the following options:

- **Display all results for the specified field**
- **Provide default value**
- **Show "Page not found"**
- **Display a summary**
- **Display contents of "No results found"**
- **Display "Access Denied"**

So, you can act like the filter isn't there (just use any other filters, fixed or contextual), provide a default (which you have done, and we'll talk more on it in a minute), hide the entire view (in other words, don't display anything if no value is specified), display a summary (which can be a count or other information; frankly I've never used this option), display the contents of "No results found" (which is sort of like hiding the view but acknowledging that the view exists), or display the *Access Denied* error (which is an option I personally hate because it implies a permission issue instead of a missing value).

Default value options

Almost always, I end up providing a default value, which is essential when you build block displays because they don't actually have a URL to get values from. Let's look at the options that are available when you select **Provide a default value**:

- **Content ID from URL**
- **Fixed**
- **Query parameter**
- **Raw value from URL**
- **Taxonomy term ID from URL**
- **User ID from logged in user**
- **User ID from route context**

Let's start out with some easy ones, and we'll come back to the more complex options.

Fixed is by far the simplest and is surprisingly handy. It is a simple, fixed value. So, if you don't have a URL parameter, you will use this value. It could be a number or a string, although you should avoid strings that have spaces or any character other than letters or numbers in them because there are rules for encoding any other character that you'd have to follow. You've seen %20 in URLs; this is a space encoded. There are encodings for every character you might use, but they make the URL really hard to read. So, if you wanted a contextual filter of the minimum asking price, the fixed default might be 100000 to only show properties with prices above $100,000. Note that the formatting isn't important to Views when passing a filter value.

Content ID from URL is equivalent to the older node ID from the URL option made more general as everything in Drupal 8 is an entity. Every page generated by a node or entity display has a URL that is something similar to /node/999, where 999 is the node number of the content. Most sites have the path module turned on, so instead of this, URLs are more SEO-friendly, such as /this-is-all-about-me. However, even though the SEO-friendly version is displayed, Drupal still knows about the /node/999 version. So, this node ID number can be used by Views as a value for a contextual filter.

The same logic applies to the last three options: the taxonomy term ID and the two user ID options. For the taxonomy term ID, if your content type has a taxonomy field, then the term ID can be looked up automatically. The logged-in user ID is the older Drupal method of looking at the user ID of the logged-in user, and even anonymous users can be thought of as logged in but with the user ID 0. The second user ID is from Drupal 8 using Symfony and it can look at how the page is generated for user information. Also, it has the option to take the author ID of a node instead of using the logged-in user.

Raw value from the URL basically counts the slashes (/) and assigns a number to what is in between each slash. The site's base URL is argument 0, but you can't use it. What's next is 1, after the second slash is 2, and so on. So, /admin/structure/types would make argument 1 admin, argument 2 structure, and argument 3 types.

Query parameters is sort of like the raw value option; only, instead of using position relative to slashes, you put a query at the end of the URL. You've seen queries and probably not paid a lot of attention to them. They are URLs, such as /admin/structure/types?harry=2&sally=4. This URL defines two query parameters: harry and sally. To have the value of the filter set to sally, you would enter it into the query parameter field. The advantage of query parameters is that you can specify them in any order, so /admin/structure/types? sally=4& harry=2 would give the same results as the first example. Leaving a query parameter off will result in an empty parameter being used by the view.

One of these options can handle almost any application you can think of. If not, Views can be extended via code to allow more options, but I can count the number of sites I've needed to do this on one hand and still have fingers left.

Default value exception options

You'll notice that under the options for default values, there is an **Exceptions** fieldset. This field lets you specify a special value that will cause the filter to pass everything. By default, it is set to `all`, so if you had the URL parameter of `/user/6/all` and the third value was used as the default for the filter, then this URL would tell the filter to show all the values, effectively disabling the filter or making it act as though the **Display all results for the specified field** option had been selected.

Value present options

Moving on to the next section, **WHEN THE FILTER VALUE IS AVAILABLE OR A DEFAULT IS PROVIDED,** you have two options. You can override the title that the view defined, using Twig syntax replacement patterns (a pair of curvy brackets instead of a single square bracket in the earlier versions of Drupal) so that you have the title indicate what is passed into the filter. I think you used this option when you did your neighborhood views but need help getting the taxonomy term to be displayed instead of the term ID.

Validation options

Also, you can specify additional validation of the value being passed to the filter. Jim canceled the filter they had been using and clicked on **Authored by** to show the validation options screen, as shown here:

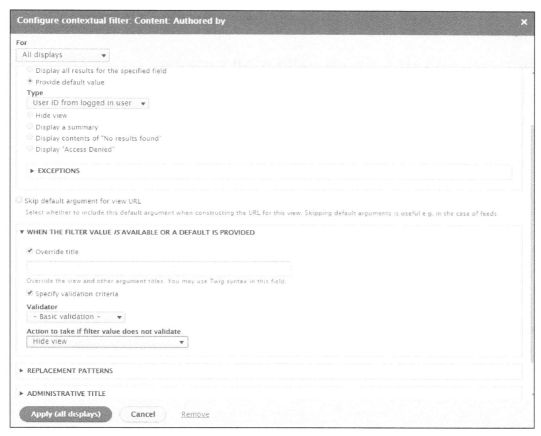

Contextual filter validation options

Most of the validation is permissions-based, so it might be easier to use the **Access** options of the view itself, but this validation can be more extensive. In the previous versions of Drupal, when Views was a contributed module and the PHP filter module was part of core, you could even put in PHP programming to do pretty sophisticated validation. Fortunately, this option isn't available as it was a security issue to have PHP stored inside a view like that. Now, for this kind of validation, you'd need to create a custom module that defines a new validation plugin. This is good news for us developers but not so good for site builders who could muddle through getting something built. But this is a tradeoff I like for the maintainability of the site.

The validation you can do through the user interface includes the options in these tables:

Non-permissions-based validation options

Validation type	What kind of validation is performed
Basic validation	There is no validation beyond what Views does for all values.
Comment	Validation can be limited to a specific comment type. Does the user have permission?
Contact message	Validation can be limited to a specific form. Does the user have permission?
Content	Validation can be limited to a specific content type(s). Does the user have permission?
Custom block	Validation can be limited to a specific block type(s). Does the user have permission?
Custom menu link	Validation can be limited to a specific menu link type(s). Does the user have permission?
Feed	Validation can be limited to a specific feed type(s). Does the user have permission?
Numeric	Is the filter value a number?
Taxonomy term ID	Validation can be limited to a specific vocabulary type(s). Does the user have permission?
Taxonomy term name	Validation can be limited to a specific vocabulary type(s). Does the user have permission?

Validation types that are not strictly permissions-based

Permissions-based validation options

Validation type	What kind of validation is performed
Action	Does the user have permission?
Base field override	Does the user have permission?
Block	Does the user have permission?
Comment type	Does the user have permission?
Contact form	Does the user have permission?
Content type	Does the user have permission?
Custom block type	Does the user have permission?
Date format	Does the user have permission?
Entity form display	Does the user have permission?

Validation type	What kind of validation is performed
Entity view display	Does the user have permission?
Feed type	Does the user have permission?
Field	Does the user have permission?
Field storage	Does the user have permission?
File	Does the user have permission?
Form mode	Does the user have permission?
Image style	Does the user have permission?
Menu	Does the user have permission?
RDF mapping	Does the user have permission?
Role	Does the user have permission?
Search page	Does the user have permission?
Shortcut link	Does the user have permission?
Shortcut set	Does the user have permission?
Subscription	Does the user have permission?
Taxonomy vocabulary	Does the user have permission?
Text Editor	Does the user have permission?
Text format	Does the user have permission?
Tour	Does the user have permission?
User ID	Does the user have permission?
Username	Does the user have permission?
View	Does the user have permission?
View mode	Does the user have permission?

Validation types that are strictly permissions-based

I have to say that a lot of the validation options you see in this list don't make a whole lot of sense to me. I suspect the list comes from some other part of Drupal and was easy to add here, so the developers took advantage of the work already done. And most of the validation options allow you to specify whether just one value is allowed or whether multiple values separated by plus signs (+) are allowed. If you will allow multiple values in the validation section, you need to also allow multiple values in the **More** fieldset that contains the two final options. The first, **Allow multiple values**, as I just said, lets you determine whether the field can have multiple values, and the other, **Exclude**, effectively negates the meaning of the filter, so instead of determining what should be included in the view, it determines what should be excluded in the view.

Options inside the More fieldset

Speaking of the **More** fieldset, it is an interesting part of the contextual filters options. Depending on the type of field being used, it might not even be displayed — for example, some Drupal fields such as the date a node is created or the original language field. To be honest, I never figured out how to predict in advance when a field doesn't have a **More** fieldset, but don't be concerned if you don't see it on occasion.

Numeric fields

For numeric fields, you will usually see two options in the **More** fieldset. The first, **Allow multiple values**, as I just said, lets you determine whether the field can have multiple values, while the other, **Exclude**, effectively negates the meaning of the filter; so, instead of determining what should be included in the view, it determines what should be excluded from it.

String fields

String, also known as text, fields are more interesting. They have a lot more options, a couple of which actually aren't in the **More** fieldset but appear right before it.

The first string option outside the **More** fieldset is **Case**. Its description says **When printing the title and summary, how to transform the case of the filter value**. Basically, this option lets you pick how to display the field, say changing the title of the page. The alternatives are:

- No transform
- Uppercase
- Lowercase
- Capitalize first letter
- Capitalize each word

The meaning of each alternative is pretty obvious.

The second string option is similar to the first, but for URLs, and it is **Case in path**. Its description says **When printing url paths, how to transform the case of the filter value. Do not use this unless with Postgres as it uses case sensitive comparisons**. Given we use MySQL in our sites, you shouldn't be using this option.

Moving inside the **More** fieldset, there are three other options.

Glossary mode

The first option inside the **More** fieldset is **Glossary mode**. Its description says **Glossary mode applies a limit to the number of characters used in the filter value, which allows the summary view to act as a glossary**. If you select another field option, **Character limit**, it appears with the description **How many characters of the filter value to filter against. If set to 1, all fields starting with the first letter in the filter value would be matched**. I'm pretty sure they mean field values and not field names in the description. This is a really interesting option because it lets you be fuzzy with your filters for strings. Say, you had a content type that had a field of zip codes, but they are stored in a text field, so a range filter isn't possible as Drupal doesn't know that the values are actually numbers. You can approximate a range search using the glossary mode and by setting the character limit to 3, which would limit the results to a single USPS **sectional center facility** (**SCF**), which tends to be focused around a community. Another use would be to use the glossary mode with a character limit of 1 on a view of titles. Then, you could build a page that shows the letters of the alphabet with each letter linking to the same view with a contextual filter of the letter. This would display all the titles that start with this letter. You could do something similar for a user list too. Pretty slick, right?

URL transformation

The second option inside the **More** fieldset is **Transform spaces to dashes in URL**. It doesn't include a description, but the use is pretty clear. If you don't select the option and have a field that might contain spaces, such as titles, when Drupal displays a page with filters or retrieves the filter value from a URL, any spaces in the value will be changed to %20. As this is hard to read, especially if you have a lot of short words, you can confuse visitors looking at their address bar. Selecting the option simply changes spaces into a URL-friendly dash.

Multiple values

The third and last option inside the **More** fieldset is **Allow multiple values**. Its description says **If selected, users can enter multiple values in the form of 1+2+3 (for OR) or 1,2,3 (for AND)**. If you don't select the option, your contextual filter is limited to a single value. Remember that this might be an issue if you are using validation and have multiple values allowed. However, it might be that you want to select more than one option; for instance, in our postal service example, if we wanted to select all the zip codes for Kansas City, we'd need three SCFs: 640, 641, and 649. We could pass this into a contextual filter using **640+641+649**. Note that I used pluses, which from the description are interpreted as OR; in other words, if a zip code limited to three characters starts with 640 or 642 or 649, the filter will display the row. The alternative is comma, which stands for AND.

You might have a filter for titles and want to select any content whose title contains both Drupal and Views, so you'd use **Drupal,Views** for this.

That's a lot about string filters, but there are lots of great options to use. There are a couple of other field types that can generate additional options that you should be aware of, even though you aren't likely to use either those kind of fields or the options.

Role and taxonomy field options

The first is a "many to one" field. It took a lot of Google searching to find out what Views means by this kind of field. The "official" description is **An argument handler for use in fields that have a many to one relationship with the table(s) to the left. This adds a bunch of options that are reasonably common with this type of relationship**. This was about as clear as mud to me, so I dug a little deeper. That's when I realized why I had never seen the options. The two examples of fields that *might* be considered many-to-one fields are roles and certain kinds of taxonomy fields. Until Drupal 8, I'm not sure I knew that Views could actually filter based on a user's role. And the requirement on the taxonomy term is that it is defined as allowing multiple values, but I noticed that the tags field of the article content type didn't generate the additional options. If you do run into a field that is considered a many-to-one field, you'll see the **Allow multiple filter values to work together**, **Reduce duplicates**, and **Do not display items with no value in summary** options. They let you define more than one filter and then link them together and have the net result determine whether a row of content is displayed. One warning from the code is don't enable both allow multiple filter values and reduce duplicates.

Null fields

The last type of field you might use in rare cases is a null field. You select it from the **Global** grouping of fields, such as text area and so on. You're probably wondering why you'd ever want a null or empty field as a filter. Think of null fields as "ignore me" fields. So, let's say you want a URL that has the word `property` in it, such as `bluedroprealty.com/property/62`, and you want to use positional contextual filters. If you just put a filter for property number, which might be the node ID, it would use the text property and not match any properties. However, add a null field above the node ID, and the filters would work the way you expect. This is the only use case I've seen in my experience. However, the null field has an option, **Fail basic validation if any argument is given**.

If you selected this option and gave it my example URL, it would fail and not select property 62. So, the only URL that would work for this case would be `bluedroprealty.com//62`. This seems like a really odd URL to me, and I can't think of why you'd want to use it, but the option is there. I have seen it used in exposed filters to keep a view from displaying until the user has selected their options, and it might be that this feature is just a result of sharing code between filters and contextual filters.

This covers everything in the contextual filter options, so does it make sense now?"

Lynn replied, "Thanks so much, Jim! It does. I agree that some of the validation options don't seem too useful, but maybe someday, I'll find a use, and there are certainly enough of them. I really appreciate you spending the time to go through this section in detail with me."

"No problem, but I need to run. We have our daily stand up in about 15 minutes, and I'd like to get a refill before heading to the office," Jim replied as he stood up and got back into line. He turned and said to Lynn, "Why don't you take a look at the **Relationships** option just below **Contextual Filters**. I think you'll find the solution to your listings by neighborhood title problem there."

Lynn was looking forward to digging into relationships.

Summary

Contextual filters are like exposed filters that take the value they are filtering by from the URL. Even though they are filters, they are maintained in the third column of the view edit screen under **Advanced**. As an alternative to passing the value via the URL, contextual filters can create a default value from information that Drupal has about the environment that the view is being displayed in, such as the node ID if it's a page, the user ID if it's a logged-in user, and so on. This ability makes contextual filters very useful for blocks.

In the next chapter, relationships will be presented. Relationships are valuable when content has entity references, which include taxonomy terms. Without a relationship, all the content can display is the ID of the entity that is referenced by the entity reference field. However, add the relationship, and all these fields become available to use in sorting, filtering, and displaying as fields.

5
Relationships

This chapter shows how to use relationships to gain access to even more data to display. Drupal's core taxonomy field stores the taxonomy ID, which isn't too useful to most site visitors; but add a relationship between the content type that uses the taxonomy and that taxonomy vocabulary, and any fields in that vocabulary become available for display, filtering, or sorting. Lynn can modify her neighborhood view to use neighborhood names instead of taxonomy IDs to filter the property list. Similarly, using the built-in entity reference, any reference field can be used to add all the fields in the referenced content to the available fields list. Entity references make it possible to show information about the realtors' along with property information. And because of relationships, we can make powerful attachment displays, such as showing the open houses associated with a group of property listings.

Fixing the neighborhood property listing title

Lynn sat down at her computer and noticed she was alone tonight. "I guess Jackson decided to hang out with the family, so I'll talk to myself."

From the Views list of views, Lynn selected her *Available Property Listing* view and clicked on **Edit**. She then clicked on **Neighborhood Page** to select the display she wanted to change.

Be careful when you are editing views that have multiple displays. More than once I've made unintended changes to the wrong display and clicked on **Save** before realizing my mistake. Then I had to change the display back to what it should be and make the changes to the right display. Another common mistake is to forget to use the override option and make changes to all displays when you really wanted to edit just a single display. Both mistakes are good reasons to use multiple views rather than having a single view with lots of displays.

Adding a relationship

Given Jim's hint that she needed a relationship, Lynn clicked on **Add** next to **Relationships**. The modal that appeared looked like the following screenshot:

Adding a relationship

Looking at this modal, Lynn thought, "That's a lot more options than I would have expected for the property content type." Scrolling through the list, it appeared that some of the options were for things she wouldn't have thought were relationships, like files associated with a node, or revisions for content. Thinking about that, it made some sense, but other options, like fields associated with other content types, didn't make any sense.

As she scrolled through the options, she settled on **Taxonomy term referenced from field_property_neighborhood** and selected it. She changed **For** to **This page (override)** so it would just impact the neighborhood display, not being certain what effect having the relationship would have on the other displays. She clicked on **Apply (this display)**. Now she saw another modal screen that looked like the following screenshot:

Taxonomy term relationship options

This modal screen only added a single option, **Require this relationship**, which had the description **Enable to hide items that do not contain this relationship**. Since she didn't want to hide anything that didn't have a neighborhood, she left it unchecked. She clicked on **Apply (this display)** again, and was back at the view edit screen.

Nothing had changed in the preview except the SQL, which looked a little more complex. Remembering that she had changed the page title in the contextual filter, she clicked on **Content: Property Neighborhood** to edit the filter's title override option. Expanding the **REPLACEMENT PATTERNS** fieldset, she was disappointed to see that it hadn't changed.

"Hmmm, I wonder what went wrong," she mused. "Maybe I have to delete the contextual filter and add it after the relationship." So she deleted the contextual filter and re-added it with the same settings as before, only to discover that the same replacement patterns were available. "Okay, just because I have defined a relationship doesn't mean that I can access the extra fields everywhere. Lesson learned. So I wonder how I can see the title?" She clicked on **Cancel** to ignore the new filter.

Relationships often add new fields

She thought a bit and decided to try adding the contextual filter one more time to see what new filter options were available at the first step of selecting the field to filter. Before adding the relationship, when she had clicked on **Add**, there weren't any taxonomy-related fields other than the entity relationship defined in the Property content type. And that field displayed as a number instead of the title as she wanted. This time, when she clicked on **Add**, she looked in the **Type** pull down, and noticed that **Taxonomy** was listed as an option. When she selected **Taxonomy**, she found that there were a number of fields available now, as shown in the following screenshot:

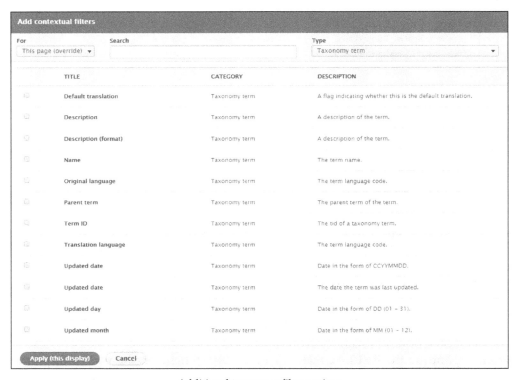

Additional taxonomy filter options

"Let's see what happens when I select **Term ID**, which would keep the same filter values." Selecting that option and clicking on **Apply (this display)** didn't change the replacement pattern options other than the actual names used, so she clicked on **Cancel** again. Trying yet again, she decided to use the term **Name** field, which is Drupal's name for the taxonomy term title. This time, after clicking on **Apply (this display)**, she saw useful replacement patterns, and entered her title override. Just before clicking on **Apply (this display)** one more time, the screen looked like this:

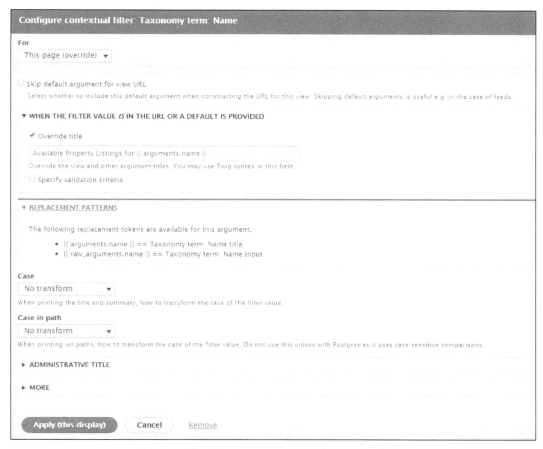

Title override with taxonomy name as the contextual filter

She clicked on the **Apply (this display)** button and entered a neighborhood name into the contextual filter field in the preview section. This time, the result looked like what she wanted, so she clicked on **Save** to save the resulting view.

Sometimes, the exact field or relationship that you need to use in either a contextual filter, or in a field display won't be obvious. It often takes a couple of tries to figure out the correct set of fields and options that will result in what you want. As long as you haven't clicked on **Save** to save the view, you can always back up and start over. However, it is a good idea, if you are not absolutely sure of what you will do next, to make sure that you have saved the view before experimenting, just in case. The truly paranoid, or safe, can duplicate the view, experiment, and then delete the copy if all goes well. Remember the maxim of computers: *save early, save often.*

Since she had changed the filter from a taxonomy term — a number — to the actual name of the neighborhood, she had to change the URLs that she had in her image map page. So she navigated to it and made the necessary edits, remembering that spaces had to be changed into %20. She discovered that any other non-alphabetic characters like periods also had to be converted and googled a chart of replacements. After checking the results, she thought, "That is more complex than I would have imagined. Maybe I should get Jim to explain relationships to me." She shot off a quick e-mail to Jim.

To: Jim

From: Lynn

Subject: Relationships

Okay, Jim. I fixed the neighborhood view to display a reasonable title using a relationship. I'm not sure I did it right, and it was really confusing. Can we get together again and you can do your great explanation of how relationships work?

Lynn noticed that Jackson had joined her while she was trying to figure out relationships. "Hi Jackson, good to see you."

Before Lynn could finish reading her other e-mails for the day, a reply came from Jim.

To: Lynn

From: Jim

Subject: RE: Relationships

Sorry Lynn, I guess I use relationships so often, I forgot they can be confusing. I'm impressed you figured out as much as you did. How about day after tomorrow before work, like we did last week?

Jackson decided it was time for Lynn to quit for the night and moved from his spot next to her monitor to lie down on her keyboard. "Okay Jackson, I get the hint."

What are relationships?

After Jim and Lynn had gotten their coffee, they sat down at a table and Jim got out his pad of paper. "Let's take a look at the relationships between the various content types you have defined on your site." He drew a diagram that looked like this:

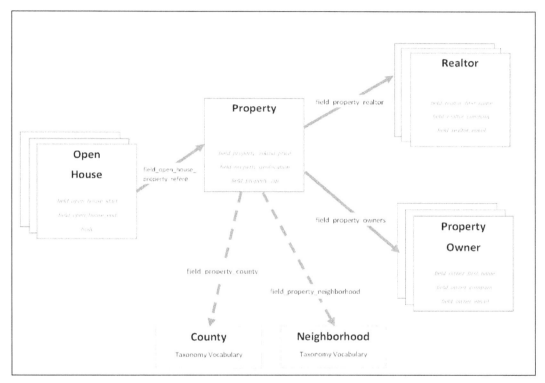

Blue Drop Realty content type relationships

Blue Drop website relationships

"Okay, your site has four main content types: Property, Realtor, Property Owner, and Open House. They are related to each other, so the `field_property_realtor` in Property references the Realtor nodes, the `field_property_owners` in Property references the Property Owner nodes, and the `field_open_house_property_refe` in Open House references the Property nodes.

There are two other entity references that Drupal created for you when you put taxonomy term fields in your content type. This is a bit of a change from Drupal 7, but mostly in terminology since everything in Drupal 8 is an entity, whereas in Drupal 7, taxonomy terms were still partly special.

Entity references are stored in Drupal as entity IDs — for a lot of content, this is the same as the node ID, which you are familiar with from Drupal 6. When you create a view of a content type that includes entity references by default, the only value available to the view is that entity ID, although for some purposes, such as creating filters or sorts, Drupal will go ahead and automatically, and invisibly, create a relationship so you can use them for simple cases without knowing about relationships. That's why, you can create a taxonomy filter based on a taxonomy term name, but when you move to a contextual filter, you can't. Drupal automatically converts the term names that you select to match against, back into the entity IDs that would be stored in the content type for the view.

Each content type has a number of fields defined — I've listed a few examples for each of the content types you defined. In addition to the fields you defined, there are some that are automatically created by Drupal, like whether a node is published, promoted to the front page, when the last update was made, and so on. Similarly, for taxonomy terms there are the term names, which you found, as well as other internal fields like the various multilingual fields — such as the language field — and the description field, which is the taxonomy's version of the default body field.

But to actually use any of these fields beyond the entity ID, you need to tell Views to create the relationship explicitly. That keeps views that don't use related fields faster by avoiding a lot of database queries that aren't needed. If you were one of our developers who know SQL, I'd be saying making relationships optional saves several SQL JOIN statements, which can be time consuming if the databases aren't designed well.

Relationship "direction"

Note that in my diagram, I have drawn the relationships as arrows to indicate there is a direction. That's because, in most cases, you want to create entity references from one content type to one or more of another content type — in your case, from Property to Realtor or Property Owners. A single property will have one or more realtors who are responsible for the listing, and may currently be owned by one or more people or companies. These are defined as one-to-many relationships.

Reverse relationships

Of course, you could have defined the relationship the other way, the way you defined your Open House content type, where the open house has the relationship to the property. This assumes that you are going to have more than one open house for a given property, otherwise you might as well include the fields in the Property content type instead of defining a many-to-one relationship. That's fine if all your views will be of Open Houses, and you just want to include the property information for that open house. But if you start including Open House information on property listings, then as the numbers grow large, you'll notice the view slow down quite a bit.

The direction of the relationship also impacts how you create the content. You need to have the referenced content defined before you can use it in a referenced field. For realtors, that is pretty easy — they don't have that much turnover in their sales group, so once you set them up, you are set. With property owners you'll just need to remember to create the Property Owner nodes before you create the Property node, at least until either the Entity Connect or the Inline Entity Form modules have stable releases for Drupal 8 — then you can add property owners while editing a property.

As much as possible, you should follow the arrows on the diagram, in other words you want to go from the property to the realtor. Going the other way is possible in SQL, but it is relatively "expensive". Following the arrows can be done using indexes, but going the other way requires loading all the values and then sorting through them to figure out which ones you want. Right now, you wouldn't notice the difference, but load your site up with a hundred thousand properties and as many owners, and you'll see the numbers get pretty big.

When you defined the relationship between Property and Open House starting in the open house, I guess you were thinking of something like: you do listings of properties, then you come back and set up open houses. That makes sense, and it might be easier to add open houses after the fact with that organization, rather than adding them and then editing the property. Long term that might not be the best option, we should see if we can get one of Entity Connect or Inline Entity Form working, and switch the relationship before you get a lot of data.

Automatic reverse relationships

Back to relationships and Views, Drupal automatically creates that back link, or reverse relationship, when you create entity types. But as we just discussed, you should avoid them as much as possible for content types that are going to have lots of nodes.

When you add a relationship to a view, in most cases, Views will offer you two options, which you may have seen when you added, say, realtors to your property listing view. Those two options are:

- **Content referenced from field_property_realtors**
- **Content using field_property_realtors**

The first option is from the property to the realtor, the second is the reverse relationship.

You might be wondering: if we're doing a view of properties, why even offer the reverse relationship? Some views start to get really complex, and it gets pretty hard to know which way you might want to go. So Views tends to offer options, even if they don't necessarily make a lot of sense, just to be really flexible. You've already seen this when adding fields to display. You can be building a view of properties and have it offer fields from the Article content type. Of course, if you pick a field like that, you'll realize that the result is always blank since the field doesn't have any way to decide what data is appropriate."

Again, I repeat the advice given in the *Debugging* section of *Chapter 1, Up and Running with Views*. If you add a field, or use it as a filter or relationship, and the results are blank or don't make sense, make sure you have selected the right field. Many fields have the same name or similar names, such as the default Body field. But displaying the Body field of an article in a view of properties will usually result in blank results.

"Does that make sense?" Jim asked after the explanation.

"It does, thanks," was Lynn's reply.

"Then let's add the listing realtor and their phone number to your property listings to show what we just learned."

Adding realtor information to the property listings

Jim pulled up the site on his computer and logged in. Selecting the property listing view, he started to edit it. Clicking on **Add** next to **RELATIONSHIPS** and entering `realtor` into the search field, he got the following display:

Adding a relationship to realtor

"Okay, from what we just discussed, which one should we use?" Jim asked.

Lynn replied, "The first one, **Content referenced from field_property_realtors**."

"Good," Jim replied. "Although, either would actually work here. In most cases, Views can work with either, it's better to pick the right one. I'd say the realtor should be on all these displays, don't you?"

"Sure."

He selected **All displays (except overridden)** in the **For** selection list and clicked on **Apply (all displays)**.

On the next modal, Lynn asked what the option **Require this relationship** meant.

"**Require this relationship** forces the SQL query generated by Views to limit the results to just those rows in the table that actually have the relationship. Again, if you were a developer, I'd explain it switches from a LEFT JOIN to an INNER JOIN. Generally, I'd recommend you require the relationship unless you have a reason not to. That will help prevent mistakes in configuring a view from displaying random, incorrect data."

Adding new fields

Jim selected the **Require this relationship** option, and clicked on **Apply (all displays)**.

Back at the view edit screen, he clicked on **Add** to add another field to the fields being displayed in the **Fields** section of the first column. At the field selection modal, he typed Title into the search field, resulting in a display like this:

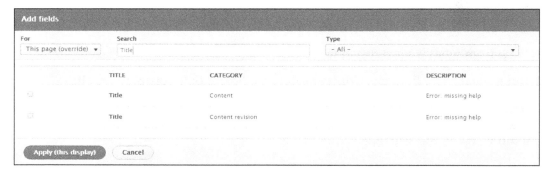

Adding the title of a related field to the fields to display

"You'll see that while there are two **Title** fields listed, one is for **Content** and the other is for **Content revision**. There aren't two Title fields, one for property and one for realtor. That may look confusing, but remember that, for Drupal, the Title field is the same. It's the content type that decides what data should be selected. So let's pick the **Title** from the **Content** category." He selected **All displays** from the **For** selection list and clicked on **Apply (all displays)**.

The next modal looked like this:

Adding the title of a related field to the fields to display

"This screen should look very familiar with the addition of a new selector right at the top of the options—**Relationship**. This is where you can tell Views what relationship to use. I'm actually going to leave it set at **Do not use a relationship** to show you what happens if you don't change this option. We'll also just accept all the other defaults for now; I think they will be fine, and if you want to tweak them later, you can do that on your own."

He clicked on **Apply (all displays)** and returned to the view edit screen. What was displayed looked like the following screenshot:

Preview results with no relationship

Scrolling down, he showed Lynn the preview results and asked, "So what do you see here?"

Debugging when you forget to specify the relationship

"The **Title** results in the first column are the same as the **Title** results in the last column. Where's the realtor's full name?" Lynn asked.

"Good catch. Since we didn't specify a relationship, Views assumed we wanted the title from the View Type that we used when we created the view, in this case, Property. So let's go back and change the relationship to **field_property_realtors: Content** in the **Relationship** field." He quickly made the edit, and when he clicked on **Apply (all displays)**, the following was displayed:

Preview results with relationship

"That's what we want!" Lynn added, "It's amazing how a single setting can make the difference in what is displayed. I would never have figured this out by myself."

Jim added the realtor's phone number and left the **Relationship** fieldset to no relationship; the resulting preview showed blanks instead of the phone number.

"Even though it was clear when we selected the field that the field was from the Realtor content type, Views doesn't know that and, to keep everything clear, you need to select the relationship every time you use a field from the other content type."

> If you don't get the results, and especially if you get blank results, check if you set the **Relationship** field on fields coming from other content types.

He went back, changed the field to include the relationship, and removed the label from the field. He changed the label on the second **Title** to **Realtor** and the label on the first **Title** to **Address**. Jim then changed the settings on the table format to combine the realtor's name and phone number into a single column to make the table a bit more compact.

"There, that looks pretty good. We'll take care of making the various neighborhoods look the same when we theme the site using CSS."

"That's great, Jim. Thank you for the explanation and showing me how the **Relationship** field can completely change what is displayed." Lynn replied.

"My pleasure. I've got to run to today's stand-up. Try another view when you get time to practice what we discussed. Maybe now is the time to try a real challenge. You haven't done an attachment display yet. Why don't you see if you can figure out how to display the open houses associated with a property list, and see how it reacts to the exposed filters? I'll give you one hint—the attached display needs to be in the same view as the display it will be attached to."

"Thanks again, and I'll do my homework this week."

Adding an open house attachment display to the property listings view

As Lynn sat down at her home desk to work on her attachment homework, Jackson took up his usual position next to her monitor. Lynn gave him a scratch and said, "Okay Jackson, ready to attack adding an attachment to our selectable property listing view?" Lynn logged into the development site and navigated to the *Available Property Listing* view edit screen.

Once there, she clicked on the **Add** button in the display area and selected **Attachment** from the pull-down that appeared. What she saw after adding the attachment display was this:

Available Property Listing edit screen with attachment display

Scanning the options that appeared from the master display that was hidden, Lynn noticed there was a contextual filter. "That's not supposed to be there Jackson. I must have forgotten to select the **Apply to this display** option when I added it to the neighborhood display. I see why Jim suggests using several separate views instead of a single view with multiple displays. It is easy to make mistakes like that. I'm surprised the other displays still work." Making a note to fix the other displays when she had time, she clicked on the neighborhood contextual filter. In the options modal that appeared, she selected **Apply to this display**, then clicked on the **Remove** link at the bottom to delete the filter from this display.

Defining what to attach a view to

Continuing her scan of the edit screen, she noticed that the options for path and menu had been replaced by options for the attachment display. After clicking on the **Not Defined** button next to the **Attach to** label, she checked the Selectable Page in the modal that appeared. "I guess we can attach this display to more than one display Jackson, but let's keep this simple." She made a note to ask Jim about the implications of selecting more than one, then clicked on the **Apply** button and moved on to the next option: **Attachment position**.

Lynn wanted the open houses to appear after the property listings, so she clicked on **Before** and selected **After**, then clicked on **Apply**.

The next option, **Inherit contextual filters**, had defaulted to **Yes**. Lynn decided that was because she had a contextual filter that came from the master display. Since she had deleted the contextual filter for this display, she clicked on **Yes** and changed it by unchecking the **Inherit contextual filters** option.

Below **Inherit contextual filters** was **Inherit exposed filters**. Lynn wanted to show open houses only for properties that were shown on the page, so she clicked on the default **No** and changed it to **Yes**.

The **Access** option was the same as the Selectable Page display, so she left it the same.

Adding the relationship

"I guess we need a relationship to the Open House content type, don't we Jackson?" Jackson had gone to sleep and barely raised an eyebrow to acknowledge Lynn's question. She clicked on **Add** in the relationships section. In the modal that appeared for selecting what relationship to define, she typed open and saw the options shown in the following screenshot:

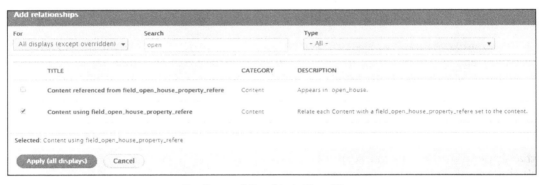

Creating a relationship to Open House

She knew that when Jim added the relationship to the realtor, he had mentioned that the first option was for cases where the entity reference field was in the content type that the view was based on, in this case, Property. Since she hadn't changed the way Open House was defined despite Jim's suggestion, she figured that, in this case, she would need to use the second option—for which the given description was: **Relate each Content with a field_open_house_property_refere set to the content.** So she checked that option, and before clicking on **Apply**, changed the **For** to **This display**.

In the options modal, she decided that since she only wanted to display open houses for the properties being displayed, she should check the **Required** option as the description said **Enable to hide items that do not contain this relationship**. She clicked on **Apply (this display)**.

Cleaning up what is displayed

Having added the relationship to Open Houses, she decided to tackle what was being displayed. When she looked at the fields listed, she realized that they were all for the property and almost none were applicable to the open house listing she was creating now. Lynn also realized she'd need to delete all but the **Title** field, which was the address of the property. She didn't relish the idea of selecting each field, changing the **For** to **This Display**, and then clicking on **Remove** to delete the field from this display for six different fields. Then she remembered that when she was rearranging the fields originally, there was a **Remove** link. So she clicked on the **Rearrange** option in the **Fields** section. What she saw looked like the following screenshot:

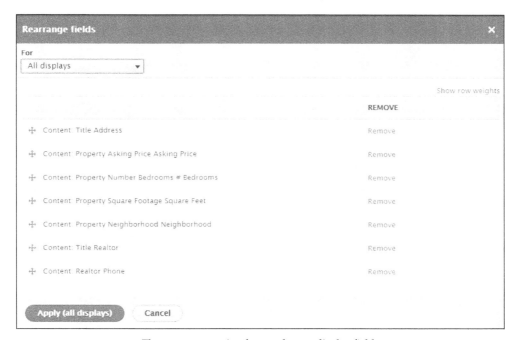

The rearrange option for attachment display fields

Working from the bottom, Lynn clicked on the **Remove** link next to all the fields shown, except **Content: Title Address**. Remembering to change the **For** from **All displays** to **This display (override)**, she clicked on **Apply (this display)** and was left with a single field showing in the **Fields** section.

Adding Open House fields to display

Then she clicked on **Add** to add the open house fields that she wanted. In the search field, she put open, and from the resulting list, she selected **Content: Open House Start**. Curious to see what would happen if she didn't specify the relationship, she skipped the field and completed the rest of the options. Clicking on **Apply (this display)**, she looked at the preview. As she had expected, the start column was blank. She clicked on the field name and selected **field_open_house_property_refere** as the relationship. After clicking on **Apply (this display)** again, she didn't like the formatting option she had picked. "I don't want to display the date twice, one for start and one for finish." So she changed the **Date format** to HTML Date. The options looked like the ones shown in the following screenshot:

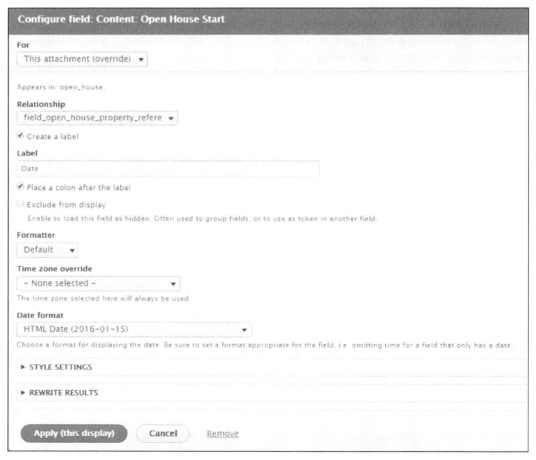

Open house start date field options

"Okay, that added the date; now let's add the start time." Lynn clicked on **Add** and used the same sequence as for the date, even selecting **Content: Open House Start** as the field. The only difference was that before clicking on **Apply (this display)**, she selected **HTML Time** as the **Date Format**.

To add the end time of the open house, Lynn again added a field, but after entering open into the search field, she selected **Content: Open House End** for the field to display. She also selected the same options as the starting time, including using **HTML Time** as the **Date Format**. When she clicked on **Apply (this display)**, she saw that the preview looked like the following screenshot:

Open house attachment preview

"Okay, I don't like the formatting of the dates and time, but the order and basic information is right; I can fix the formatting in a little bit." Lynn switched to the Selectable Page display by clicking on the button with that label at the top of the view edit screen and saw a preview that looked like the following screenshot:

Selectable Page with open house attachment preview

"That looks like what I expected. I wonder if it works like it too?" Lynn clicked on **City Center** in the neighborhood exposed filter and clicked on **Apply**. The listing of properties changed to show only those in the City Center, but the list of open houses didn't change at all and showed some open houses for properties that weren't shown in the property listing above it. "Hmm, I think there is something wrong with my new attachment."

Adding exposed filters to the attachment

Lynn switched back to the **Attachment** display and looked at the view definition. Not seeing anything obvious, and feeling thirsty, she got up and went into the kitchen to get herself a drink of water. Coming back to the screen, she sat down and looked again. "Hey Jackson, I don't see the exposed filters in my attachment view. I wonder if I need to define them in the attachment too?"

She then added each filter, making sure to select **Expose the filter** and use the same options as she had on the Selectable Page. Several times, she switched back and forth to the Selectable Page display to see what options she had used for each filter. "I have a feeling there is an easier way to accomplish this," Lynn remarked to Jackson as she finished.

If you have a display and you are attaching another display to it using attachment, it is generally easier to use the duplicate as an attachment rather than adding an attachment option, which will duplicate the master display. The duplicate of a display option is on the pull-down at the same level as the **Display name** option, as shown in the following screenshot.

Options for duplicating a display are on the right-hand side of this example

That way any customizations for that display, such as filters and relationships, are copied to the attachment. Then it is a matter of making the changes you need for what you are displaying. Duplicating the display is particularly handy when you use the inherited exposed filters or contextual filters options.

Switching back to the Selectable Page display only brought Lynn disappointment; changing the exposed filters didn't update her attachment. She decided to work on the formatting of the output, and ask Jim later about why the exposed filters didn't work.

To fix the formatting of the dates and times, Lynn knew she needed new date and time formatting options. From her existing site, she knew that they were defined in a configuration screen. Going through the Drupal menu **Manage | Configuration | Regional and language | Date and time formats**, she clicked on the **+Add format** button near the top of the page and added her new formats for dates and times using the information provided in the link in the format description, **See the PHP manual for available options**. "That seemed easier than in Drupal 6. It seemed like you had to define the PHP format in one place then define the date or time format in another. Now it appears to all be on the same screen."

After getting the date and time to look the way she wanted, she wanted something to set the open houses apart from the listings above them. So back at the **Attachment** display edit screen, she clicked on **Add** next to **HEADER** under **PAGE SETTINGS** in the center column of the display edit screen. Scrolling through the list of available fields, she decided on a Text area. In the resulting modal, she typed:

```
<h2>Upcoming Open Houses</h2>
```

This was to make her header format as a second level heading for the attachment. Switching back to the Selectable Page display one more time, the attachment looked OK but still didn't seem to update when the exposed filters were applied. She clicked **Save** to save her work and decided to take a quick look at the Selectable Page itself to see how the view with the attachment would look as a page. Absentmindedly, she selected **City Center** from the neighborhood exposed filter and clicked on **Apply**. What she saw looked like the following:

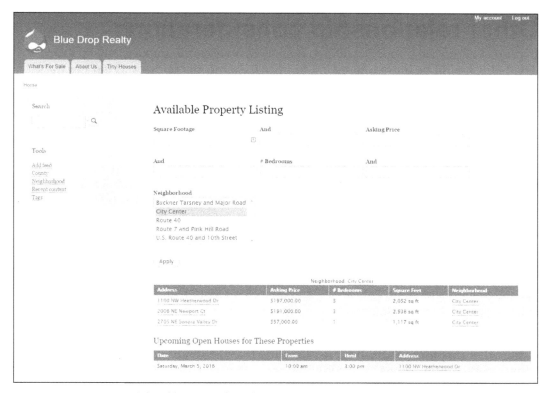

Selectable Page with working open house attachment filters

"What do you know, the exposed filters really are working, just not in preview. I wonder why, I guess I'll ask Jim."

Views preview doesn't always work exactly as expected. A lot of the time it will be because you are working in the administration theme and CSS formatting or other functionalities of the theme aren't being applied. Sometimes it is JavaScript that isn't being applied during preview. If you think something should be working a certain way and isn't, but otherwise your data looks like it is there, it might be worth looking at the actual use of the view (a page or block) to see if it is just a limitation of the Views preview capability or a real issue with your display. Just remember to save the view since changes made to a view and not saved don't show up outside the view edit screen.

Other relationship considerations

Lynn picked up the phone to call Jim. Seeing Lynn about to make a call, Jackson decided it would be more interesting to prowl around the house and left her desk with a leap.

"Hi Jim."

"Hi Lynn, what can I do for you tonight?"

"I got the attachment with upcoming open houses working on the main Selectable Page display that I've been building. I ran into an odd problem though. I kept trying different things to make the list of open houses match the list selected by the exposed filters, but it just wouldn't work. I was about to give up and ask you to meet me, when, for no reason at all, I saved my work and decided to see what the page looked like otherwise. Oddly, the filters that didn't work on the open house listing in the preview worked fine on the actual page."

"That doesn't seem right. Let me try that on a clean install, and if I see the same behavior, we'll file an issue on Drupal.org about it. What else?"

"I noticed when I was attaching my new display that I could select more than one of the other displays to attach to. I'm learning that flexibility usually comes at a cost. What are the implications of attaching to more than one display?"

"Great question. Actually there isn't much in the way of cost in terms of processing. My only warning would be to make sure the filters on the attachment and all the displays it is attached to are the same. As you may have discovered, having a mismatch can cause a filter to not be applied correctly, resulting in answers that are counterintuitive—either results you don't expect in the attached display or results you want not showing up. As we've discussed, as much as possible, I recommend you build a separate view for each display anyway, since it keeps things straight and makes changes easier. But, of course, you can't have an attachment for more than one display if you have them in separate views."

"I saw that tonight. When I created the attachment display it inherited a contextual filter from the master display. That didn't seem right, so I'm guessing that when I added the contextual filter for the neighborhood display, I forgot to change the **For** option from **All displays** to **This display**. I'm amazed that the other displays still work."

Jim was a little slow to answer; Lynn could hear him typing and figured his instant messenger had interrupted him. "Okay, I can see that in your view. You got lucky that when you added the contextual filter, you selected—or didn't select since it is the default—the **Show all results** option for when the contextual filter isn't in the URL. That's the same as not having the filter. Had you gotten clever with that setting, you likely would have broken other displays."

"Now I see why you keep suggesting separate views for different displays. One last thing: I noticed that as my displays got more relationships, the displayed SQL query got longer and longer, especially for the open house attachment."

Picking the right View Type

"Picking the right View Type is actually important because of relationships. Relationships are mostly one directional. So if you have a View Type of open house, you can have a relationship to a property, and Drupal knows how to make the related data available to you. Views can do a reverse relationship lookup, but you really want to make every effort to get the View Type set up right, since working backwards puts a big strain on your database. My advice is: start with the right View Type. Generally, you will use the type that has references to other entities, rather than the type that has references to it."

Lynn's next assignment

Jim concluded with, "I think you have gotten a good understanding of relationships. That's amazing work on your part. So what is next on your list?"

Lynn replied, "I think I'd like to add a featured property carousel like we have on our current site and maybe a map of where the properties are."

"Then it's time to install some Views add-on modules from Drupal.org. On the map, you are going to find that our Drupal 6 standbys, location, and GMap are still missing a Drupal 8 release, even development. That's why I put the Geolocation field module on your development site. It has a limited Views option built in, not as powerful as GMap, but hopefully good enough. Do you need help picking or installing the modules?"

"Let me try on my own. It looks like I can install them right from the user interface, which is a nice change from Drupal 6 when you had to install everything for me. I can't tell you how much I appreciate your help and patience with this project."

"No problem, let me know when you need more help."

Summary

The first relationship added to the *Available Property Listing* view was for the neighborhood taxonomy. In previous versions of Drupal, taxonomies were handled differently, but in Drupal 8, they are just entity references. Extending the taxonomy case to entity types defined in custom content types, the property listing was enhanced to include the listing of realtor(s) names and phone numbers, which are stored in a Realtor content type, separate from the Property content type being displayed. That showed that even though the **Title** field was used twice in the display, adding the relationship to the second use displayed realtor names instead of property addresses. Finally, an attached display showed how to use a reverse relationship to show open houses for the properties displayed with the Selectable Page display. Inheriting exposed filters and relationships that use a field that is itself defined by a relationship were demonstrated.

The next chapter adds more Display Formats using add-on contributed modules. Views in Drupal 7 has almost 600 add-on modules; Drupal 8 already had 65 when it was released in November 2015. Many more will be released in the months that follow the official release of Drupal 8. Using add-on modules, we can add a slideshow, or rotating carousel, as easily as enabling the module, installing the JavaScript library it uses, and defining a very simple view. Just as easy are JavaScript accordions that open and close when clicked, revealing content. Finally, we'll add a Google map to the site using geolocation data stored in each Property content type. These are just three of the add-on modules available, but they add a lot of power to your site building.

6
Add-on Modules

Views has a very extensible architecture and there are a large number of contributed modules that extend the functions of views to allow many different types of displays. At the time of release of Drupal 8, a search of Drupal.org modules using the category Views resulted in 65 modules; not all are extensions and some, such as CTools, are support modules that are tagged for Views, because they are necessary for older versions of Drupal. That number climbed to 85 with Drupal 8.0.2. The number will continue to grow as modules are converted to Drupal 8 by their authors or the community. By comparison, at the time of release of Drupal 8.0.2, there were 608 Drupal 7 modules in the Views category.

In this chapter, we'll install and configure Views Slideshow to create a rotating carousel of featured property images. Then we'll build a very simple Google map using the views formatter integrated in the Drupal 8 version of the Geolocation module, since the traditional "go to" module for mapping, GMap, hasn't released a Drupal 8 version yet. Next, a view using Views Accordion will show how to change the long properties available listing into a visually compact accordion display, which opens sections as they are clicked. Finally, we'll quickly look at three additional add-on modules for Views that have Drupal 8 releases — Views Field View, Views Infinite Scroll, and then a Calendar display using a view defined by the Calendar module (which uses the Views Template module to help create the view).

Adding a rotating carousel to the front page

As it started to snow outside, Lynn sat down at her computer. Jackson decided that the warmth of the monitor was a good idea and nestled into his usual spot for a nap while Lynn worked.

Lynn logged into her development site and started to work on building her rotating carousel of featured properties. First she went through the list of properties and decided on half a dozen that she wanted in the carousel. She edited each property and checked the **Featured** field option, following it up by clicking on **Save and keep published** to save the changes.

Install the Views Slideshow Module

Next she installed the Views Slideshow module by going to the project page on Drupal.org at `http://drupal.org/project/views_slideshow`. Lynn scrolled down to the **Downloads** section, found the recommended release for Drupal 8 (at the time of writing — 8.x-4.0), right-clicked on the **tar.gz** link, and copied the link location. Switching to her development site, she navigated to **Extend**, then clicked the **+Install new module** button at the top of the page. On the next page, below **Install from a URL**, she pasted the link location that she had copied from the project page. The installation screen looked as follows:

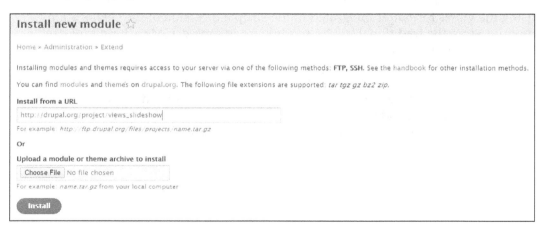

Installing the Views Slideshow module.

Note that how you install modules can vary depending on your development workflow and hosting environment. Not all hosting environments allow direct installation of modules, Acquia Cloud being a notable one. Moreover, your team development workflow might have a different way of adding a module (some teams only use Drush make files to create the site). The method described here is one way, but requires your server to support the option.

After clicking on the **Install** button and once Drupal had installed the new module, she chose the **Enable your new module** option to return to the modules page. Scrolling down the page, she enabled the Views Slideshow and the Views Slideshow Cycle modules. She remembered Jim explaining it for her old site that the Views Slideshow Cycle module was a submodule of Views Slideshow which was installed at the same time.

Add a new view

Then she went to the Views listing page (**Manage | Structure | Views**) and clicked on the **+Add new view** button. "This display is different enough from the property listings that it is an easy decision to make it a new view", she thought to herself, not wanting to wake up Jackson by talking to him as usual.

On the **Add new view** page, she named the view **Featured Properties**, selected show **Content** of type **Property**, and left the default sort order, since in a carousel, there isn't a lot of context for an order. She checked the **Create a block** option and left the block title as the default. She changed the Display Format to **Slideshow** and the information displayed from **titles** to **fields**. Lynn also changed the **Items per block** option to **0** to display all items and left the **Use a pager** option unchecked.

Just before clicking **Save and edit,** the page looked like this:

Adding the featured property view as a block

Add fields

At the view edit screen, Lynn added the featured image field by clicking **Add** in the fields section, typing `featured` into the **Search** field, selecting **Property Featured Image**, and then clicking on the **Apply (all displays)** button.

In the **Configure field** modal, she selected **Large (480 x 480)** as the image format and left all the other options at their default value; so the screen now looked like this:

Property Featured Image field options

Adding a filter

Lynn clicked on the **Apply (all displays)** button. Next she added a filter, clicking on **Add** in the filter section and typing `featured` into the **Search** field. This resulted in a large number of options as shown in the following screenshot:

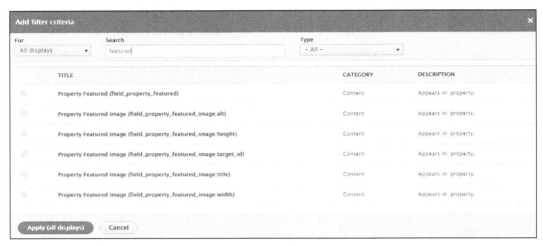

Filter options for the keyword Featured

Lynn thought to herself (Jackson was still asleep), "That's a lot of filter options. I can see most of them are for the featured image property; it's interesting that you can filter by the properties of the image itself. But all I need is the featured option of the property to be checked." She clicked on the first option, **Property Featured**, and clicked on the **Apply (all displays)** button. At the **Configure Filter Criterion** modal, she selected the **Is equal to** and **True** options and clicked on **Apply (all displays)** one more time.

Debugging slide rotation

Looking at the preview of the view so far, Lynn noticed that the slides weren't advancing. This time, rather than spending a lot of time wondering if she had done something wrong, she clicked on **Save** and proceeded to add the resulting block to the front page.

This is another case of the Views preview not displaying what will ultimately show on the site. Unlike the exposed filter display, which was likely a bug, Views has always had a limitation that some JavaScript and virtually no CSS is loaded into the preview, so the visual display of a preview won't show. Similarly, when GMap is released for Drupal 8, or the way it currently works in Drupal 7, the map that results from a view isn't displayed. That can make debugging hard. Is the right data really being output? I have occasionally switched the format from the slideshow or GMap to table just to see what data is actually coming out, switching back to the format I want once I get the data right.

After configuring the blocks page, flushing caches, and viewing the front page, she saw that the block was displaying the featured houses.

However, the images were still not rotating.

Installing the jquery.cycle library

Lynn messaged Jim using HipChat. A little while later, Jim messaged back that the library that Views Slideshow Cycle needed was missing and he'd have to install it for her. When Jim had installed the jquery.cycle library found at `https://github.com/malsup/cycle/downloads` in the `/sites/libraries/jquery.cycle` directory, he messaged Lynn back. She went to the front page, cleared caches, and lo and behold, the properties were cycling to the next property every few seconds.

A lot of Views add-on modules require PHP or JavaScript libraries. Sometimes they are explicitly clear about how to install those libraries. Sadly there isn't a strong standard for dealing with add-on libraries. Almost all modules now put the libraries into the `/libraries` directory, but a few still have you put the library into the module's own directory. Moreover, not every module is consistent about where they put any messages about the library being missing, or incorrectly installed. Many put it on the module configuration page, some put it on the status report page, and a few, like Views Slideshow here, put it in the **Settings** modal. So, sadly, you might need to look around and/or Google for help. Most likely your first indication of a problem is when the view doesn't display what you expect or with the functionality that you are expecting.

Switching back to the view's edit screen, Lynn was curious to know where the setting for the time that each property image was shown was. She figured it would be one of the settings in the slideshow format, so she clicked **Settings** next to **Slideshow**. Scrolling through the list of options, she noticed a lot of options for the slideshow, but she didn't see the timing. Going back through the options again, this time more slowly, she noticed an option, **View Transition Advanced Options**. Clicking on that option displayed a number of additional fields, as shown in the following screenshot:

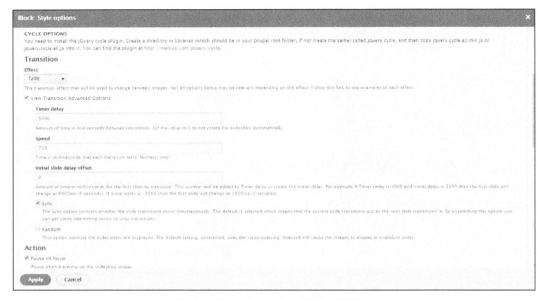

Finding the cycle rate in a hidden fieldset

Many Views add-on modules have evolved to have a lot of options. For these modules, the options map to parameters in the PHP or JavaScript library that the module is interfacing to Views. You will likely need to track down the documentation for the underlying library to understand the options offered by the module. Alternatively, you can poke around the options and try promising ones until you find the one you want. Be aware that sometimes, enabling a checkbox will show a lot more options, like in the preceding example. The good news is that the modules expose a lot of options, but the bad news is that they rarely make the relevant ones obvious. A little research with Google can often pay off if you need more than defaults.

jquery.cycle options

Under **View Transition Advanced Options**, there are two possibilities: **Timer Delay** and **Speed**. **Timer Delay** is the length of time each property will be shown, in milliseconds—so divide by 1,000 to get seconds. On the other hand, **Speed** is how long the transition will take, again in milliseconds. The default values are 5,000, or 5 seconds per property, and 700, or 0.7 seconds for the transition itself. Those values seemed okay to start off, but Lynn made a note of where to go if she wanted to change them later. Clicking on **Apply**, she checked the rest of the view edit screen to make sure she had the view configured like she wanted for the site. Under **BLOCK SETTINGS** in the center column, she changed the block name to **Featured Property Carousel** to make it easier to know the block's purpose on the block layout screen. She also changed the **Allow settings** option to **None** by clicking on **Items per page**, clearing the checkbox, and clicking on **Apply**. The rest of the options on the edit screen seemed okay, so she clicked on **Save** to save the view. After clicking on **Save**, the screen looked like this:

Views Slideshow view edit screen after saving

Turning off her computer for the evening, Lynn said, "Come on Jackson, let's celebrate by watching a movie with the family."

Mapping content

The next morning at the office, Lynn called Jim. "Hi, Jim."

"Hi, Lynn. What can I do for you?"

"I got the featured properties carousel working pretty easily last night."

"That's great. Some of the modules have made great progress migrating to Drupal 8."

"I was going to add a map, but I didn't see a Drupal 8 version of the GMap module that we have on our current site. How are we supposed to build maps in Drupal 8?"

"Some modules have been slow to join the Drupal 8 party. GMap and Location, two modules that have been the mainstay of Drupal 6 and 7, don't appear to have made any progress towards a Drupal 8 version. Leaflet might be an alternative that is just getting a Drupal 8 version ready. Right now it is listed as alpha, but it might be in a better shape than they feel it is. One of the reasons we suggested you use the Geolocation module as an alternative to the Location module was that it comes with a relatively simple Views integration built in. It doesn't have the configurability of GMap, but it might be sufficient for your purposes. Why don't you give that a try? It's already enabled on your site—you just need to define a view using the Geolocation CommonMap Views Display Format."

 At the time this book was being written, Geolocation for Drupal 8 was at version 1.5, which includes the Geolocation CommonMap views display option. If you don't see the option, you might be using an older version of the Geolocation module.

When she got home that night, Lynn got a cup of tea and went into her home office to try creating a map. Jackson followed her and took up guard in his usual place. "So you're going to join me tonight Jackson?" She gave him a nice scratch.

Creating a view for the map

Logging into the development site, Lynn navigated to the Views listing page and clicked on **+Add new view**. Lynn called the new view **Property Map**, creating a view of **Content** of type **Property** sorted by the default **Newest first**. Moving down the page, she checked the box to create a page, changing the title to **Available Properties Map**. She changed the **Display format** option to **Geolocation – CommonMap**, and changed from **teasers** to **fields**. Since she wants all the properties to be displayed on the map, she changed **Items to display** to **0**, which disabled Drupal's pager. Looking over the page before clicking on **Save**, she saw the following:

Available properties map view setup

She clicked on the **Save and edit** button to move to the view edit screen.

"So what do you think Jackson, what do we need to create a map?" I don't see one on the preview yet. I wonder if the CommonMap display formatter has options that have to be set." Clicking on the **Settings** link next to **Page Geolocation – CommonMap**, she found the modal that opened as follows:

CommonMap settings page without a geolocation field

Adding the geolocation field

"Okay, it looks like I need to add a geolocation field to the display to give the map something to display." She clicked on **Cancel** and then on **Add** next to **Fields**. Entering location into the **Search** field in the field selection modal, she selected **Property Geolocation** and clicked on **Apply (all displays)**. In the field configuration modal, she selected the **Geolocation Lat/Lng** formatter option, as shown next, and clicked on **Apply (all displays)**:

Geolocation field settings

Lynn was about to give up and save the view, thinking that the preview wasn't going to work again, when a Google map appeared with markers for the properties on it. The view looked like the following:

Available properties map view with preview

"Jackson, that was downright easy!" Lynn exclaimed, scaring Jackson who thought something had attacked her and hissed. "Sorry to scare you fella, but I just built a map in like 10 minutes. Except that it is wide and skinny. Let's see if Jim is on HipChat." Before opening the instant messenger, she clicked on **Save**.

[Lynn] You there?

[Jim] Yes, what can I help you with?

[Lynn] Can you look at the Property Map view on development and tell me why my map preview is wide but really short? I looked at the page and it looks the same, so it isn't the preview biting me again.

[Jim] Sure, give me a second to look.

There was a pause that felt a lot longer than it actually was. Jim started typing:

[Jim] I see the issue. GMap controls the height and width via settings in the view. It looks like this formatter does it with a tiny bit of CSS in the module. I tweaked that CSS just to let you see it can be changed, but when we build the site for real, we'll put this CSS in the theme.

[Lynn] Wow, that looks perfect. I'm impressed how fast I built this map – only about 10 minutes.

[Jim] That's great work. And it looks like a handy capability in the module. Anything else?

[Lynn] While I've got you, I don't like the way Views does paging of data when you have too much data. Is there anything that works like Facebook, where more appears when you scroll down?

[Jim] I think the community can help you. Install the Views Infinite Scroll Module and see if that works for you. You don't have a lot of data on the site yet but, if you set paging to every three or four items, it should give you an idea of how it works. Good luck, and let me know if that is what you're looking for.

[Lynn] Thanks Jim and sorry to disturb you at night.

[Jim] No problem, I was doing some reading on my computer anyway. Have a good night.

[Lynn] You too.

Doing away with pagers – creating an infinite page

"Okay, Jackson, the evening is still young. Let's try playing with Views Infinite Scroll," said Lynn. She searched on Drupal.org for the module, found it at `https://drupal.org/project/views_infinite_scroll`, and copied the `.gz` file link URL. Lynn used Drupal's built-in module installer to add it to her site. She then enabled the module and navigated to the Views listing page again. "I should bookmark this page—I spend so much time here."

As an experiment, she decided to use the *Available Property Listing* view that she had used so often. She clicked on **Edit**, and on the view edit screen, she made sure she was on the **Page** display at the top. She clicked the **Duplicate Page** button on the right and changed the name of the display to **Infinite Scroll**.

Since she was changing the pager, she presumed the module added some new options to the **PAGER** settings, so she clicked on **Full**, next to **Use pager**. The resulting modal looked like this:

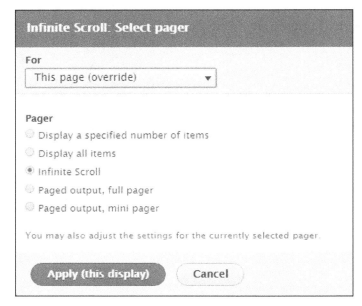

Selecting Infinite Scroll pager

She changed **For** to **This page (override)** and clicked on the **Apply (this display)** button. Since she hadn't set the options for the new pager, the next modal that was displayed for the options looked like the one seen in the following screenshot:

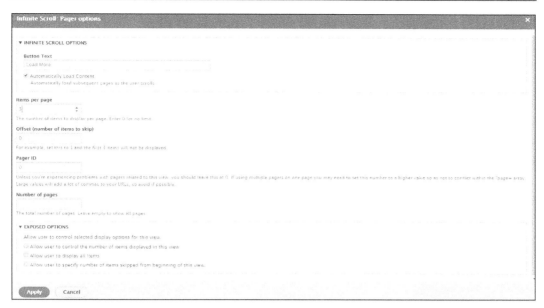

Selecting Infinite Scroll options

Remembering Jim's message, Lynn changed the **Items per page** to **3** and selected the **Automatically Load Content** option. By clicking on **Save (this display)**, the resulting preview showed the first three properties. As she scrolled down to get a good view of the preview section, she noticed the Drupal loading circle and then saw that her three properties had turned into six. "That's pretty slick!"

She tried scrolling down again and three more properties appeared. Just for fun, she scrolled up and nothing happened. "I guess this is a one-way feature, Jackson. This display is cute, but I just got an idea for one that would be really slick." She clicked on **Save** to save her changes and navigated to the Views listing page one more time. She clicked on **+Add new view** again to create a new view.

Creating an infinite scroll property image gallery

On the new view page, she named the view **Infinite Scroll Property Gallery** and set the view settings as show **Content** of type **Property** sorted by **Newest first**. She checked **Create a page**, titled it as **Available Property Gallery**, set the path as **property-gallery**, the Display Format as **Grid** of **fields**, and the number of items to display as **4** with **Use a pager** checked. The setup looked like this:

Creating a property gallery view

She clicked on **Save and edit** to move on to the view edit screen. There she clicked on the **Settings** link next to **Format Grid**, set the **Number of columns** option to **2**, and checked **Automatic width**. She left the rest of the settings at their default values, as seen in the following screenshot:

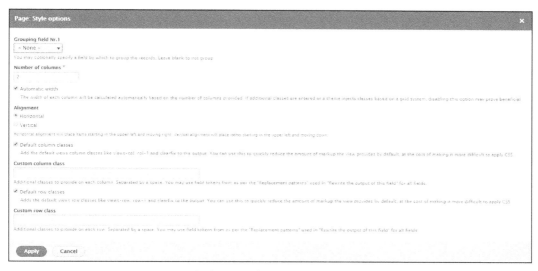

Grid settings for property gallery

Next, she added the following additional fields:

- **Content: Title**
- **Content: Property Featured Image**
- **Content: Property Asking Price**
- **Content: Property Number Bedrooms**
- **Content: Property Square Footage**

She set the field options to display like she wanted, setting the **Property Featured Image** field as the image formatter using the **Large** image style and linking it to the content.

Finally, she set the page to **Infinite Scroll** with the same settings she had used before, especially the **Automatically Load Content** setting. Clicking on **Apply**, she waited for the preview to refresh and was pleasantly surprised with the result. As she scrolled down, additional groups of four properties were displayed. "That's a great result Jackson." Jackson got up thinking it was time to play, "Just a minute Jackson, I need to save the view and tell Jim."

The resulting view looked like this screenshot:

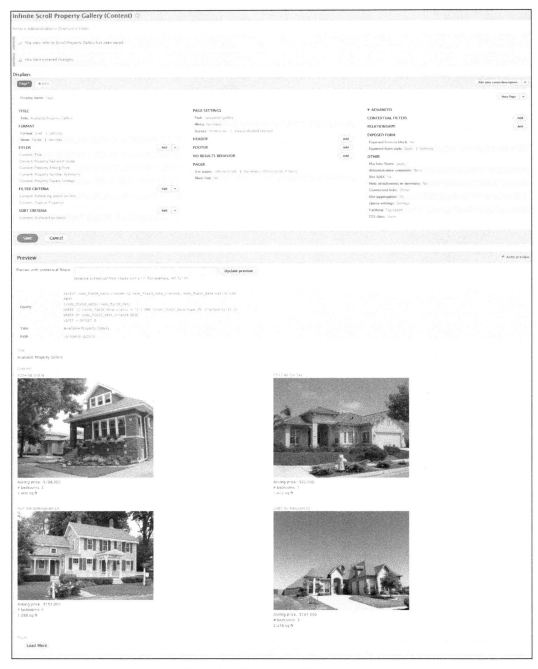

Property gallery view with preview

[Lynn] Take a look at /property-gallery

[Jim] Sweet, that's a great way to display properties for the casual browser. I'm impressed you came up with that so fast.

[Lynn] Thanks, off to play with Jackson.

Lynn turned off her computer, picked Jackson up, and headed to the family room to play.

Expandable accordions hide and show content

On Lynn's existing Drupal 6 site, Jim had put up a **Frequently Asked Questions (FAQ)** section, where Lynn had put in a lot of information about Blue Springs, the surrounding area, and activities that potential homeowners might be interested in.

As the list got longer, Jim enabled a feature in the FAQ module that turned the questions and answers into expandable questions. When a visitor first visited the page, all that showed were the questions. Once a visitor clicked on a question, the area between that question and the next one would expand and the answer was displayed.

Lynn had learned they were referred to as accordions. When looking for the carousel module, she noticed a module called Views Accordion and decided to try and see if she could create a more full-featured FAQ page. She navigated to `https://drupal.org/project/views_accordion` and installed the Drupal 8 version of the module.

Her existing FAQs consisted of questions and answers only. Lynn thought it would be great to include a picture too. She created a new content type called FAQ that used the **Title** field for the question, the **Body** field for the answer, and added an **Image** field for the picture.

After entering enough data to test the view, Lynn was ready to starting building it. She made sure that the Views Accordion module was enabled and set up a new image style called **FAQ Picture** that cropped and scaled the image to 1000 by 200 to create the banner look she envisioned.

Then she navigated to the Views list screen and clicked on **+Add new view**. On the next page, she named the view **FAQ** and selected a view showing **Content** of type **FAQ**, sorted by **Title**. After that, she created a page with the title **Frequently Asked Questions** and the path setting as **faq**.

Under **PAGE DISPLAY SETTINGS**, she selected **jQuery UI accordion** as the Display Format and selected a display of **fields**. She set the number of items to display as **0**, which disables paging and displays all the FAQs on a single page. She also added a menu link on the main navigation menu, labeled **About Blue Springs**. Before clicking on **Save and edit**, the page looked like this:

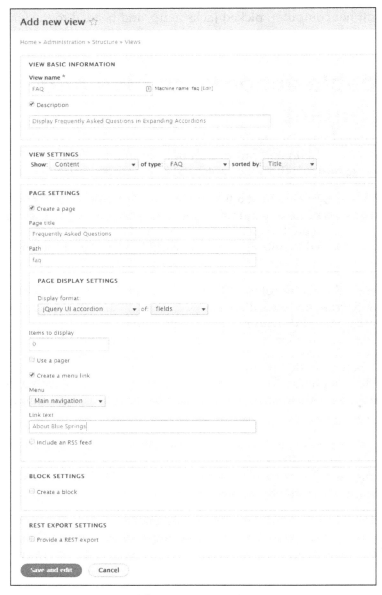

FAQ view creation settings

On the view edit screen, Lynn added the FAQ picture field, setting the **Image Style** to **FAQ Picture**. The settings for that field looked like this:

FAQ Picture field settings

After clicking on **Apply (all displays)**, she added the body field to display the answer. Looking at the preview, she decided that she wanted the FAQs to start off as all collapsed. To change the settings of the accordion, she clicked on **Settings** next to **jQuery UI accordion**, which is the Display Format. Scanning the **Settings** page, she noticed the first prompt: **IMPORTANT: The first field in order of appearance will be the one used as the "header" or "trigger" of the accordion action.**

"That works for us Jackson. I want the title to be the header since that's the question being asked." Jackson ignored her.

She changed **Row to display opened on start** to **None** and selected the **Allow for all rows to be closed** option below it. Lynn noticed that a number of options for the jQuery library providing the accordion functionality, including the transitions, were configurable. She left all those options at their defaults and clicked on **Apply**.

This time, the preview acted the way she was hoping for. It started off by displaying just the list of questions. Clicking on one opened the answer to the question, along with the scaled picture that she wanted. Clicking on that question again closed it. Or clicking on another question closed the first one and opened the second. Before she clicked on **Save**, the view looked like the following screenshot:

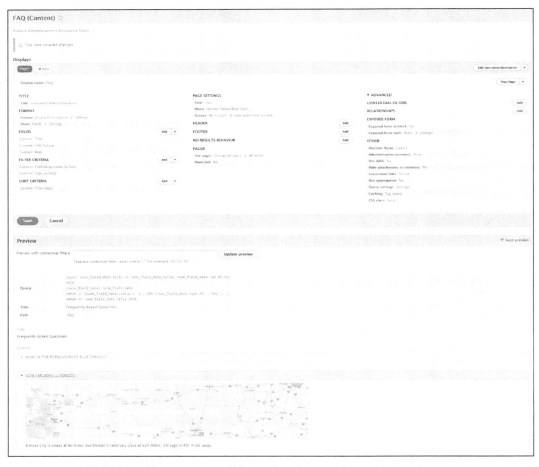

FAQ view with preview, note this map is an image and not an interactive map

"I think I'm getting good at building interesting displays using Views and contributed modules Jackson," Lynn said as she reached over and gave Jackson a scratch. He purred—it was just the kind of attention he was hoping for when he followed her into the office that evening.

Putting one View inside another

"It's still early, how about we try one more before calling it quits?" said Lynn. Jackson was too busy enjoying his stomach rub to pay attention to her. She gave him a pat and said, "Okay, for my last feat of amazing displays, let's see if we can use that module Jim suggested—the one that lets you embed one view in another as if it were a field. I think we can use that to do something really interesting like a property display that includes open houses within the property listing. What was the name of that module?" Looking at her notes, she remembered it was Views Field View. Navigating to `http://drupal.org/project/views_field_view`, she downloaded the module and installed it on her development site.

Lynn didn't see any documentation on the project page and no documentation page linked to the project page. So she downloaded the `.zip` version of the module and expanded it on her computer to look for a `readme.txt` file. Sure enough, there was one that contained the following description:

> This module allows you to embed a View as a field in another View.
>
> The View in the view-field can accept argument values from other fields of the parent View, using tokens.
>
> Here's how:
>
> 1. Before you can add a view-field to a "parent" view, you must create a "child" view.
> 2. Add arguments to that child view. The parent view will be passing argument values to the child so that the child knows what to display. No other settings are necessary, but validators and "argument not present" could be set.
> 3. Create a "parent" view, if not already existing.
> 4. Add child view (Global:View field). The field must be toward the bottom of the field list, or at least underneath the fields that are going to be used as arguments. (E.g., "node id" might be used as an match between the parent and child views, so put the "node id" field before your Global:View field in the list.)
> 5. Select which View and Display to use for the child data (will require doing this in 2 steps - the field must be saved before the display selection is available).

6. Find which tokens are available by looking at the "Replacement patterns" list right below the Arguments setting. Type the token replacements, in order, separated by a comma, as the arguments for that view field. These values will be passed to the child. Make sure each field you are passing as an argument is completely clean, as in: no label, no formatting, nothing that would pass into the argument other than the desired text or number.

Creating the child view

From the readme.txt, Lynn knew she needed to create a view of the open houses for a single property and that view should have arguments, also known as contextual filters, for the parent view to pass to the child view. She didn't know what kind of display she needed and decided to use a block and see what happened. For the contextual filter, she decided that the proper filter would be the **Open House Property Reference** field, which she configured. When she had constructed the view, it looked like the following:

Open House child view with preview

Creating the parent view

With the child view built, Lynn decided to duplicate the Infinite Scroll Property Gallery view into a new view, which she called Infinite Scroll Property Gallery With Open Houses. She could have just as easily added another display to the original view, but decided that since this was a new add-on module, which she didn't have any experience with, she'd play it safe and create a view just for it. Moreover, having a dedicated view meant that she didn't have to keep selecting to override the all display options as she added the open houses.

On the edit screen for the new view, she clicked **Add** to add a new field for the view. From the `readme.txt` file, she knew it would be a global field option, so she selected **Global** for **Type**. The resulting field selection list was narrowed to just a handful, the one she wanted was called **View** as shown in the following image:

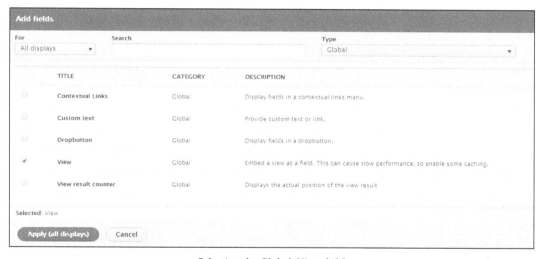

Selecting the Global: View field

When she clicked **Apply (all displays)**, the configuration modal for the field was displayed, and it looked like this screenshot:

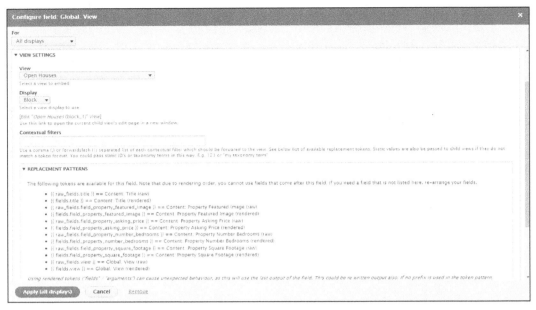

Global:View field configuration options for Open Houses view

Under **View**, she selected the **Open Houses** view from the list of views. Under **Display**, she selected **Block**, the other option being **Master**. She thought, "I guess it didn't matter what kind of display I created for the child view, this is letting me select which display I want to use." When she got to contextual filters, she read the help text and opened the replacement patterns. She had set the contextual filter on the Open House view to Open House Property Reference, which, she remembered Jim saying during his session on relationships, was actually the node ID of the entity being referenced—in this case the property node ID. Looking through the list of replacement patterns, she didn't see a node ID.

Debugging the configuration

"Okay, Jackson, I think we need to add a node ID field to this view." She clicked on **Apply (all displays)** to save the open house view field and clicked on **Add** to add another field. She selected **Node ID** and checked the **Exclude from display** option in the field configuration modal. Then she clicked on **Apply (all displays)**, followed by the **Global:View** field to add the node ID. She still didn't see it listed. "That's right Jackson, I have to have a field above the one I'm editing for it to appear in the replacement patterns."

She clicked on **Cancel** and then selected the **Rearrange** option for the fields. She dragged the **Content: Node ID** field above the **Global: View** field, and clicked on **Apply (all displays)**. This time when she went to the **Global: View** configuration options, the node ID showed up in the replacement patterns. She copied `{{ fields.nid }}` into the **Contextual filters** field and clicked on **Apply (all displays)**. When she checked the preview, she could see that the Open Houses had appeared for one of the properties. "Success, Jackson. Come take a look!", Lynn cried out as she grabbed Jackson and held him in her lap. Juggling Jackson and the mouse, she clicked on **Save**. The view and the preview looked like the following screenshot:

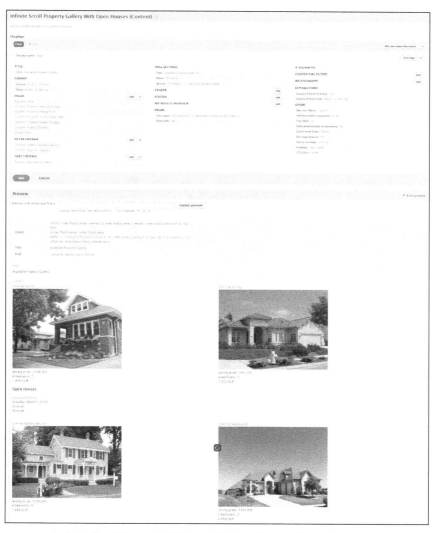

Infinite Scroll Property Gallery with Open Houses view and preview

She held Jackson so he could see the screen. "See Jackson, it makes me so excited that I could create that kind of display." While Jackson didn't seem impressed with the computer screen, he was happy to be held. With Jackson still in her lap, she instant-messaged Jim.

[Lynn] Take a look at the Infinite Scroll Property Gallery With Open Houses at /property-gallery-open-house.

[Jim] Very impressive. Amazing what you can do with Views and a couple of contributed modules.

[Lynn] True. But I'm not satisfied with how the open houses are showing up. Is there a way to format them differently?

[Jim] You could rewrite the field output. Have time for coffee this week? Then I can show you how.

[Lynn] Sure, how about Thursday morning before work, at the usual place and time?

[Jim] See you there.

Adding a calendar of open houses

The night before meeting Jim at Starbucks, Lynn decided to do one more view using an add-on module. She had seen sites with a nicely formatted calendar of events and wondered if she could do the same for her open houses. Going to `https://www.drupal.org/project/project_module`, she selected **Core compatibility** as **8.x**, **Module category** as **Views**, entered `calendar` into the **Search Modules** field, and clicked on **Search**. The first result was the Calendar module, which sounded exactly like what she wanted.

Installing the Calendar and Views Templates modules

She clicked on the title link, which took her to `https://www.drupal.org/project/calendar`. Reading the project page, she noticed that the Drupal 8 port is not feature-complete because of a difference in the way Drupal 8 date fields and the Drupal 7 contributed module Date handled dates. She didn't think that the issue mentioned was important to what she wanted to do for a calendar display, so she installed that module on the development site. When she tried to enable the module, Drupal wouldn't allow her to select the module due to a dependency on the Views Templates module, which wasn't installed.

So she navigated to `https://www.drupal.org/project/views_templates`, downloaded, and installed that module on the development site. Then she could enable both the modules.

Adding a calendar view

When she navigated to the Views listing page (**Structure | Views**), she noticed a new button next to **Add new view**, that said **Add view from template**. Knowing that the calendar module required Views Templates, she assumed that she needed to use the new button. Clicking on **Add view from template** made the following screen appear:

Add view from template	
Home » Administration » Structure » Views	
Name	Description
Custom block Changed Calendar	A calendar view of the 'Changed' field in the 'Custom block' base table
Comment Post date Calendar	A calendar view of the 'Post date' field in the 'Comment' base table
Comment Updated date Calendar	A calendar view of the 'Updated date' field in the 'Comment' base table
Feed Authored on Calendar	A calendar view of the 'Authored on' field in the 'Feed' base table
Feed Changed Calendar	A calendar view of the 'Changed' field in the 'Feed' base table
Feed Last import Calendar	A calendar view of the 'Last import' field in the 'Feed' base table
Feed Next import Calendar	A calendar view of the 'Next import' field in the 'Feed' base table
Feed Queued Calendar	A calendar view of the 'Queued' field in the 'Feed' base table
File Created Calendar	A calendar view of the 'Created' field in the 'File' base table
File Changed Calendar	A calendar view of the 'Changed' field in the 'File' base table
Content Authored on Calendar	A calendar view of the 'Authored on' field in the 'Content' base table
Content Changed Calendar	A calendar view of the 'Changed' field in the 'Content' base table
Content Field Open House End on Calendar	A calendar view of the 'Open House End' field in the 'Content' base table
Content Field Open House Start on Calendar	A calendar view of the 'Open House Start' field in the 'Content' base table
Content Field Property Listed Date on Calendar	A calendar view of the 'Property Listed Date' field in the 'Content' base table
Taxonomy term Updated date Calendar	A calendar view of the 'Updated date' field in the 'Taxonomy term' base table
User Created Calendar	A calendar view of the 'Created' field in the 'User' base table
User Updated date Calendar	A calendar view of the 'Updated date' field in the 'User' base table
User Last access Calendar	A calendar view of the 'Last access' field in the 'User' base table
User Last login Calendar	A calendar view of the 'Last login' field in the 'User' base table

Calendar templates available for a new view, add links have been cropped off

"Wow, Jackson, look at all the options for calendars. I can't imagine using most of them, but I assume that like many Views options in Drupal 8, they come from applying a rule to what is available, and a large list comes back whether the options make sense or not." Jackson didn't seem very interested in what she was saying, as he was playing with the wires on her desk.

Lynn scanned the list, and deciding that the **Content Field Open House Start on Calendar** made the most sense, she clicked on the **Add** link on the right side of the screen. The views templates module displayed a screen that looked like this:

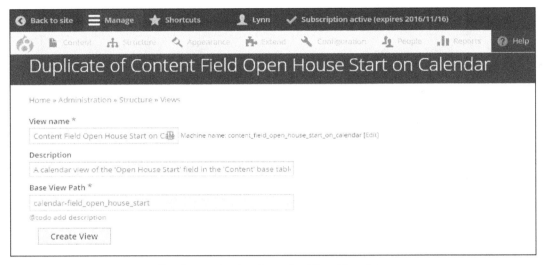

Creating a calendar view using Views Templates

When Lynn clicked on the **Create View** button, the module made many substitutions and left Lynn looking at the view edit screen with the message, **You have unsaved changes**. The field settings looked reasonable, so she clicked on the **Save** button to save the view. She clicked on the **View Page** button and was taken to a page that looked like this:

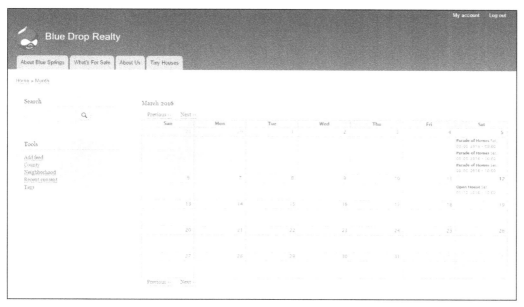

Initial results of a calendar view

Lynn said, "Jackson, that was quick and easy, but I don't like what is displayed on the calendar days. Instead of the title of the open house, which is often Open House, I'd like the address, which is the title of the property. And I want just the start time to show, the date is redundant given the calendar display."

Adding a relationship to properties

Lynn knew that in order to display the property title, given the way she laid out the content types, she'd need to specify a relationship. Clicking on **Add** next to **Relationship**, she entered open into the **Search** field and saw the following screen:

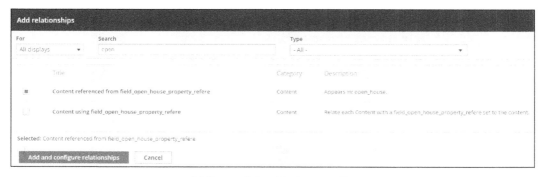

Adding a relationship to properties

Since the open house content type had a property entity reference field, she knew that she should select **Content referenced from field_open_house_property_refere**. Having established the relationship, she clicked on the **Content: Title** field which displayed the following:

Changing the title field to use the property title (address)

She changed the **Relationship** pull down to use the **field_open_house_property_refere** as the reference and clicked on **Apply (all displays)**.

Lynn then clicked on the **Content: Open House Start** link to edit the field settings. She changed the **Date format** option to **HTML Time AM/PM** and clicked on **Apply (all displays)**.

Final view adjustments

Looking at the preview, she decided to put the time first, so she clicked on the **Rearrange** pull-down instead of **Add** and dragged the start time field to be first before clicking on **Apply (all displays)**. Deciding that the preview looked reasonable, she clicked on **Save**. Then she refreshed the page to open in another tab and saw the following screen:

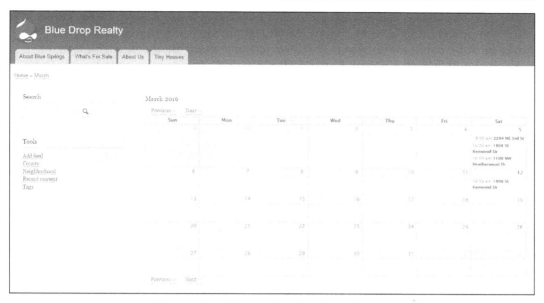

Final version of the calendar view of open houses

Jackson came over and started playing with Lynn's hands as she typed as if they were a ball of string. Lynn said, "Okay Jackson, I get the hint. I'm done, let's go join the family."

Summary

In this chapter, we have looked at using contributed modules to extend the kinds of displays that Views can create. Our first was the classic rotating carousel. Then we built a Google map using data from our properties content type. Next, infinite scrolling was used to create a gallery of properties that expands as you scroll down the page, much like Facebook and other common sites. After that, we created an expandable FAQ page that includes pictures using the Views Accordion module. Then we used Views Field View to insert a list of open houses into a view of properties, including the open houses on the property they went with instead of all at the end like when we used a Views attachment display. Finally, we created a calendar of open houses using the Calendar module, with help from the Views Template module. Views is extremely versatile and extendable. If there is some unique way that you want to display your content, it is likely that there is a contributed module to extend Views. While the number of contributed modules for Views in Drupal 8 is a fraction of the number for Drupal 7, similarities in the way they are structured means that Views add-on modules will be easier to convert to the architecture of Drupal 8.

In the next chapter, you'll learn how to change what is being displayed by Views using the powerful field rewriting capability. From simple formatting changes that could be done using other means in Views to powerful if-then-else formatting of content, you'll be surprised by how much you can do to adapt your output to the goals of your site. You may also be surprised at how many fields you can add to a view and enable their exclusion from the display option.

7
Field Rewrites

Up to this point, we have used Views to create different aggregations of data, displayed in a variety of ways: lists, tables, galleries, maps, accordions, and so on. We just displayed content titles, teasers, and used fields to create custom displays of data for each row of a view. Up to this point, we have accepted the formatting options provided by Views, whether to display a field label, which formats or displays the mode to use, or to turn the field into a link to the full content.

However, fields have a very flexible rewrite capability. Opening the **REWRITE RESULTS** fieldset in the field options shows what looks like six simple checkboxes. However, four of the six open up additional options when selected. Within these options is the ability to completely change what is output, from changing what the content links to through to creating a table of data. Coupled with the **NO RESULTS** fieldset, you can even create conditional rewriting options.

Linking to anything

Lynn got to Starbucks before Jim, so she got in line and ordered for both of them. "I'll have a grande caramel macchiato and the person I'm meeting will have a grande flat white." Just as the barista was finishing the drinks, Jim arrived. Lynn waved him over, saying, "I went ahead and ordered for you; I hope you want your usual."

Jim replied, "That's perfect, thanks."

They collected their drinks and sat down. Jim opened his laptop and navigated to the development site, logged in, and went to the Views listing page. "For the first part of what I want to show you, we can use pretty much any view, but let's use your property view. We can either make a duplicate of it or just remember to click on **Cancel** if we edit the original view, but a copy is always safer." He duplicated the view using the pull-down on the right-hand side of the row the content view was in and kept the default name **Duplicate of Available Property Listing** to highlight that it is a copy for testing only.

Jim then started his demonstration for Lynn.

Introducing field rewrites

"If you look at the field options for the **Content: Title** field, you'd think there isn't much you can change. But this is deceptive; when you select many of these options, you will find that there are a whole lot more fields that are hidden and waiting for you.

He showed Lynn the basic field options screen that looked similar to the following:

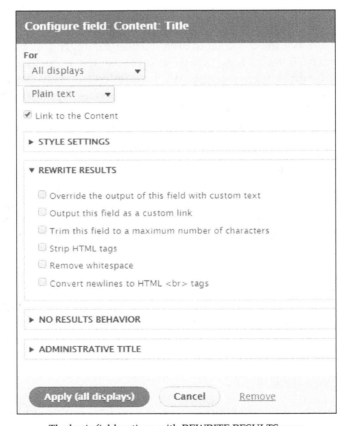

The basic field options with REWRITE RESULTS open

"I will open the field configuration screen in a separate tab rather than let Drupal open it as a modal. That will make it easier to show you all the fields on this screen without having to scroll within the default modal window." He clicked on **Cancel** to close the field options modal. Jim then right-clicked on the **Content: Title** link and clicked on **Open link in new tab**.

He clicked on **REWRITE RESULTS** to open the rewriting fieldset he planned on explaining. He also opened the **REPLACEMENT PATTERNS** fieldset to have everything displayed at once. The resulting field configuration page looked similar to the following:

Part 1 of the Content: Title field options in a separate tab with all the hidden fields displayed

Part 2 of the Content: Title field options in a separate tab with all the hidden fields displayed

Linking to content

"Let's start off with a really simple field rewrite. Actually, you've been using a limited version of it all along; it is the default option for fields, **Link to the content**. Technically, keeping this option checked will rewrite the title as a link to the content display. For most of the content, this is the node display that you configure using the display mode tab in the content type. But we often don't want to have the title display as a link, so we will clear this option.

However, what if we wanted to link the title, which in the case of properties is the address, to a PDF sell sheet for the property? This is really easy to do. If we select **Output this field as a custom link** after clearing the **Link to the content** option, a number of options will be displayed in the modal. Switching over to our show everything page, you have to look a bit to find the same option and the resulting fields as everything is showing.

The first field is the link path, for which you can have either a fixed URL or you can use Drupal tokens to create one that changes depending on the content being displayed. You'll notice the description mention **Replacement patterns** in the screenshot. If we scroll down the page, you'll see a fieldset that I've opened labeled **REPLACEMENT PATTERNS**."

Excluding from display

"Right now, there isn't much, and I doubt that we could link to the PDF file unless you were willing to upload PDF files that used the node ID as the filename. That's not a great solution in my mind. But we added a file upload field to the property content type called **Property PDF Listing**, so you can upload anything. So, to use this, we need to use the first really important trick that you will learn about doing field rewrites—how to make data available to use in the rewrite. Let's go back to the view edit page and click on the neighborhood field to see what replacement patterns are available for it. Take a look at this:

Replacement patterns for the neighborhood field

If you'll notice, there are a lot more options, including more fields. Remember the list, there will be a test in a minute. I'll click on **Cancel** and, looking at the view edit page, you'll notice that these fields are the fields that are before—or as I like to say, above, because that's where they are on the page—the field you are doing the rewrite of.

So, if we want to have the Property PDF Listing field be a replacement pattern, we can use it in our title URL; then we need to add the Property PDF Listing field and rearrange the fields so that it appears before/above the Title field we want to link to it."

Jim clicked on **Add** and added the **Property PDF Listing** field; in the options, he unselected the **Create a label** option and selected the **Exclude from display** option; and in the formatter select pull-down, he selected **URL to file**. Before clicking on **Save**, he pointed out the key changes to Lynn.

Field render as URL options

"Before I click on **Save**, let me point out some changes I made to the field options. First, I cleared the **Create a label** option as we don't want Drupal adding anything to our field output because we're using it as a URL. Then, I selected the **Exclude from display** option so that Views won't display this field. You're probably thinking that if it is excluded from the display, we can't use it, but Views makes its value available as a token, which is exactly what we want. Don't worry about remembering this; it is mentioned in the field description text. Finally, I selected **URL to file** to have Views format this field as a URL to the file, which is exactly what I want. This is actually very handy; sometimes, you won't get this and will need to build a URL from fixed text and tokens.

Let's review some of the other options for the link rewrite, although in many cases, the path field is the only one you will really need:

- The **Use absolute path** option lets you force Drupal to output the whole URL instead of a relative URL. If we hover over the preview, you'll notice that the URL appears to be an absolute path: `http://bluedroprealty.dev.dd:8083/sites/bluedroprealty.dev.dd/files/2016-02/BKD-7369390710.pdf`. But this is our browser fooling us. If we actually look at the HTML code being output, we will see that only a relative path of `/sites/bluedroprealty.dev.dd/files/2016-02/BKD-7369390710.pdf` is there. If we had selected the **Use absolute path** option, we would have seen the same URL both in the HTML code and when we hover over the link.

- The **Replace spaces with dashes** option does just what it says it does. It changes any spaces in your path into dashes. If you don't select this option, you will notice that any spaces in your filename will turn into `%20` in the URL, which is HTML's way of encoding spaces. Normally, I wouldn't recommend using this option as it can result in the URL not pointing to the file if you uploaded it as part of content. Actually, I always recommend that you tell people not to have spaces in their filenames, and this is one reason we installed the transliteration module, `https://www.drupal.org/project/transliteration`, on most of our sites.

- If you select the **External server URL** option and don't include `http://` at the beginning of the URL, Drupal will add it for you. If it is there, then it will stay there. This is a good way to make sure that `http://` is always there. One thing to note is that the code adds `http://`, which for most sites isn't a problem, but if you are linking to a site that is only SSL—that is, https—then you might have a problem using this feature if this site doesn't automatically redirect traffic. Most do, but a few, often for security reasons, don't. So, if you have problems linking off your site to an SSL site, this might be a reason.

- The **Transform the case** option will let you change the case of your URL to all upper case, all lower case, or capitalize the first character of each word, much like other places where case transformations are allowed. Again, I don't recommend using this option as some web servers can be configured to be case sensitive, so changing the case will result in *file not found* errors.

- The **Link class** option lets you assign a custom CSS class to the link so that it can be styled differently than other links on a page, perhaps adding a colored background or image to links to files.

- The **Title text** option lets you have a tooltip if you hover over the link with your mouse. It might be additional instructions about the link or something similar to *this link will open a PDF*. You can use replacement patterns and put HTML into this field, so you can get pretty fancy with it.

- The **Rel Text** option lets you add a special attribute that defines the relationship between the page you are displaying and the page the link is pointing to. This is used most frequently with JavaScript libraries, such as **lightbox2**, which lets you open pages as modals. Another use is to specify the `nofollow` rel attribute, which would tell Google and other search engines to ignore the link, perhaps because it is a paid link or something like that.

- The **Prefix text** option lets you put pretty much any text you want before the field value; for instance, in your view, the field label is put in the header of the table as a column title. If you wanted to put some other label in front of the address, you could put this here. You can use replacement patterns and put HTML into this field, so you can get pretty fancy with it.

- The **Suffix text** option lets you put text after the field value. A lot of sites like to put a small PDF icon after files that are PDF, and you could do this with this field as it can use replacement patterns and HTML, as with the other fields.

- The **Target** option lets you specify another special attribute: the target. You've probably been on a lot of sites on which, when you click on a link, it opens the web page in a new tab or window. This is done using the target attribute, in this specific case, using the target `_blank`.

If you can't get what you want with all these options, I'm not sure you should be trying to do whatever it is you are doing with the Drupal UI."

"Have I exhausted you on rewriting a field using a custom link? Or do you want to spend some more time talking about rewriting fields?" Jim asked Lynn, sensing that he had gone a bit too far with details on the simple topic of outputting a field as a link.

Lynn answered, "Let's get a refill on our coffees and keep going. You are starting to give me ideas already and I have a feeling that the best is yet to come."

Changing how fields are output

Refreshed from getting up, getting more coffee, and having a quick rundown of Lynn's son's soccer game earlier in the week, Jim and Lynn sat down at his computer again.

"Before we get to my favorite option, let's do the rest of the field rewrite options as they are really straightforward," Jim started off saying. He continued, while pointing to his screen:

- **Trim this field to a maximum number of characters** is another one of those select-the-option-and-more-options-appear checkboxes. When you select this option, you are given options not very different from when you set up a body field in a new content type. The first suboption is **Maximum number of characters**, a simple number-input field. You can limit a field to, say, 10 characters if you are using it for a button or something longer if you want a teaser-like introduction. Another option for trimming a field is **Trim only on a word boundary**, which limits the trimming to a word boundary. The trim length is then the maximum number of characters. If there are no word boundaries, usually spaces, you could trim a field to nothing. You can show that the field is trimmed with the **Add "..." at the end of trimmed text** option. Another option might be **Add a read-more link if output is trimmed**. I'd say use one or the other but not both together unless you work for the Department of Redundancy Department. The next option is important: **Field can contain HTML**. If you don't select this option and your field has HTML, such as a body field, it is very possible that you will have the opening HTML tag but not the corresponding closing tag. This option adds an HTML corrector to ensure the HTML tags are properly closed after trimming.

- The **Strip HTML** tags option lets you take a field that has HTML, again such as a body field, and remove all or most of the HTML tags, creating a plain text alternative. Or you might want to strip all the tags except paragraphs and line breaks; then, you'd use the **Preserve certain tags** suboption, putting `<p>` `<br>` in this text area.

- The **Remove whitespace** option really should be remove extra whitespace as it doesn't really remove all the whitespace. In this case, it just removes any whitespace that might be at the beginning or end of a field. It won't change any whitespace that's in the middle, which is after the first viewable character and before the last one. Whitespace is spaces, tabs, new lines, carriage returns, null characters, and vertical tabs, although you shouldn't see the latter two until you are working with data imported from another system.

- The **Convert newlines to HTML <br> tags** option is the fourth and last. In some respects, this is the opposite of the remove whitespace option. It adds HTML newlines when the contents of the field, which would usually be a text area field, has newlines. Otherwise, HTML rules say that newlines are ignored (or replaced by a space so that words don't run together), which could take a nicely formatted four-line address and "convert" it to a single-line jumble.

One last rewriting option is hiding in the **NO RESULTS** fieldset; this is **Hide rewriting if empty**. If the field is empty, you probably don't want to add extra prefixes, suffixes, or other rewriting, so you can select this option, which basically disables the **REWRITE RESULTS** option if the field is empty. This can be clever or cause problems depending on your goals. If you are combining several fields together, which we'll cover next, it might make sense to go ahead and allow what is left to be output. But then again, you could get everything set up and not output anything if it can't be a link. The possibilities are pretty interesting whether you use the option or don't."

Open house formatting

"Now, let's get to my favorite option in the **REWRITE RESULTS** fieldset, one that my developers and I use all the time. This is **Override the output of this field with custom text**," Jim continued.

"Let's switch to the attachment display on this view and look at the preview for open houses. You mentioned on HipChat that you didn't like how they looked. What would you like to see?"

"Ideally, I'd like to see the date and times together, something like Saturday, March 5, 2016 from 9:00 am until 3:00 pm," Lynn replied.

"That we can do very easily," was Jim's answer to her request. "Let me show you how."

Let's start off by hiding the first two fields in the attachment view by setting their **Exclude from display** option.

Now, we'll make a couple of small changes to the third field. First, as we hid the first two fields, the label **Until** doesn't really make sense, so let's change this to **Date and Time**.

Then, we'll open the **REWRITE RESULTS** fieldset, check the **Override the output of this field with custom text** option, and open the **REPLACEMENT PATTERNS** fieldset. Here you see some funny options, as follows:

```
{{ field_open_house_start }} ==
{{ field_open_house_start_1 }} ==
{{ field_open_house_end }} == Open House End
{{ field_open_house_end__value }} == Raw value
```

It almost looks like there are two `field_open_house_start` fields, one with an underscore one after it. This is because you have the same field listed twice. To be honest, I'm not sure why there is no text after the two equal signs; this might be a bug in Views. However, the descriptions are pretty clear and we know how we defined these two fields. The first without the underscore is the date spelled out. The second with the underscore is the start time. The `field_open_house_end` field is the ending time in the same format as the start time, `field_open_house_start_1`.

Take a look at this:

```
{{ field_open_house_start }} from {{ field_open_house_start_1 }} until
{{ field_open_house_end }}
```

If we put this into the **Text** field, it'll display exactly what you want."

Jim clicked on **Apply (this display)** and they looked at the preview.

"That looks great, Jim, and it was as easy as you'd said it would be. Let's see what the page it is on looks like," Lynn responded.

Jim clicked on **Save** to save the results, then on the selectable display, and then on the **View Selectable Page** button to navigate to the page, which looked similar to the following:

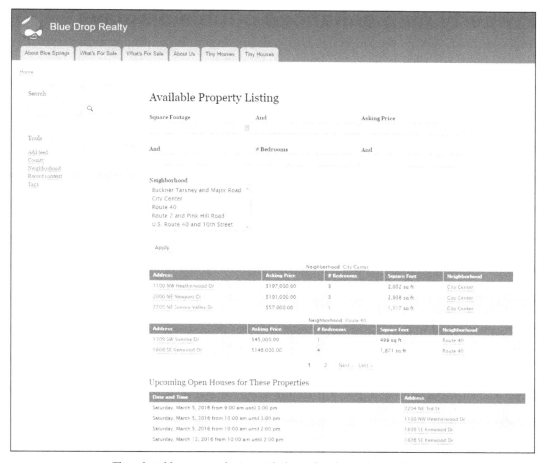

The selectable property listing with the updated open house display

If you are familiar with Drupal 8 theming, you'll recognize the replacement patterns in the previous example look like Twig `print` statements. In fact, they are. Actually, I accidentally discovered that anything you can put in a Twig template can be put into the **Override the output of this field with custom text** field. As an example, try putting the following Twig statements into your **Override the output of this field with custom text** field and look at the preview of that field (I used the Title field):

```
{% for letter in 'a'|upper..'z'|upper %}
    * {{ letter }}
{% endfor %}
```

Property map enhanced bubble displays

Jim continued, "Okay, we did one, so how about something a little more complex? Do you have any idea what you'd like to change now?"

Lynn's answer was, "Can we make the bubbles that pop up on the map show more information, such as the asking price, number of bedrooms, and square footage?"

"Sure, and to show that you have been listening, why don't you show me how you'd do this?" Jim responded, as he turned the computer to let Lynn use it.

"Okay, I'm up for the challenge. First, to navigate to the map view, we've got a backup of the database, so I'm okay with making the changes," Lynn said. Then, continuing to talk through her actions, she went on.

"The **Geolocation - CommonMap** Display Format only allows a single field, currently set to the property title/address as its **Title source** field, so let's see whether we can make this title display all the information I want."

Adding fields to the display

"First, I will need to add the asking price, number of bedrooms, and square footage fields to the view, so I'll do that now." Lynn clicked on **Add**, selected the fields one at a time, and set their options as if she were going to have them displayed, but in addition, she set the **Exclude from display** option. "I added labels for the asking price and number of bedrooms, but I think with the suffix *sq ft*, this is pretty obvious.

Now, I need to rearrange the fields, so my three new fields are first on the view. Given that I'm going to rewrite them and they are hidden, I presume they don't need to be in any order as long as they appear before the title field."

Rewriting several fields into one

"Now, I will edit the **Content: Title** field by clicking on its link. There, I will open the **REWRITE RESULTS** fieldset and select the **Override the output of this field with custom text** option. I'll expand the **REPLACEMENT PATTERNS** fieldset, which shows:

```
{{ field_property_asking_price }} ==
{{ field_property_number_bedrooms }} ==
{{ field_property_square_footage }} == Property Square Footage
{{ title }} == Title
{{ title__value }} == Raw value
```

I presume that I want the regular title and the other fields. It's interesting that the first two don't have descriptions like the one you did. So I'll copy and paste my four field patterns into the **Text** field, ending up with the following:

```
{{ title__value }}
{{ field_property_asking_price }}
{{ field_property_number_bedrooms }}
{{ field_property_square_footage }}
```

That should be it, so let's click on **Apply (all displays)** and see what happens."

After the map loaded in the preview, she clicked on one of the markers. What she saw looked similar to the following:

A preview map showing the title bubble that isn't formatted correctly

"Hmm, this isn't what I expected. What did I do wrong, Jim?"

Jim replied, "I think the location of the bubble is a side effect of the map in preview, so I would not worry about that for now. But the rest of your problem is straightforward."

Using HTML to format the rewritten field

"First, when you use fields in rewrites, most of the field options, other than the basic formatting options, are ignored. So the labels you set up would only get used if you actually displayed the field. When you think about it, this makes some sense; you don't want labels showing up when you don't want them, and they are easy to add back in.

Second, you are actually creating HTML to display. Remember that HTML doesn't show whitespace, extra spaces, or new lines when it renders. So you'll need to add explicit line breaks using the `<br/>` HTML tag. While you are at it, I think it might look a lot better if you made the address stand out a bit. You might try surrounding this field with the `<h3>` and `</h3>` tags. The `<h3>` tags have an implicit `<br>` tag, so you won't need one there.

So, why don't you update your rewrite coding and see whether you can apply these changes?"

"Thanks! I learn something every time I do new things," Lynn replied as she clicked on **Content: Title** to edit the field options. She ended up with:

```
<h3>{{ title__value }}</h3>
Asking price: {{ field_property_asking_price }}<br/>
# bedrooms: {{ field_property_number_bedrooms }}<br/>
{{ field_property_square_footage }}
```

"This looks perfect; let's see what they look like on the actual page," Lynn said excitedly, as she clicked on **Apply (all displays)** to save the changes and look at the preview. Clicking on **Save** to save the edits to the view, she then clicked on the **/property-map** link in the preview section to navigate to the page. Clicking on a couple of the map markers, she said, "It's amazing how easily we added all this information. Take a look:"

A section of the property map page showing enhanced title bubbles

Jim said, "This is nice. I have to say that the result rewriting of Views is one of my favorite features. It lets our developers and site owners get just about exactly what they want without any custom code or theme template modifications."

"I know that it's been a long session, but do you have time for just one more demonstration? This one will make you a Views ninja."

"Why not, do you want a refill?" Lynn replied.

"I don't think so; another coffee and I might not be able to type," Jim answered.

If-then-else conditional rewrites

Jim continued, "There are times when you'd like to display one of two different fields depending on some condition. Almost always, when we hear that a client wants to do something like this, we start planning on custom code to implement it. Many of these would be really hard to implement in Views, but some are of the form that if I have information in field X, then display it and otherwise display field Y. These kinds of requests can be handled within Views using the **REWRITE RESULTS** and **NO RESULTS BEHAVIOR** fieldsets."

No results options

"We haven't really covered the **NO RESULTS BEHAVIOR** fieldset, which looks similar to this when expanded:

No Results Behavior options

This is pretty straightforward. If a field is empty, you can create alternate values using pretty much the same tools you have for rewrite results. Now that you understand rewrite results, you know what is possible in the **NO RESULTS BEHAVIOR** field.

There are a couple of options beyond the alternative value field labeled **No results text**.

Working back from the end display we want, we already discussed the last option, **Hide rewriting if empty**. If selected and if the field is empty, then Views won't even try to output the rewriting text. This is good if you are assembling a link and don't have all the data or you are doing additional formatting; there's no reason to output a bunch of HTML code that wraps literally nothing.

Right above this option is a similar option, **Hide if empty**. Where **Hide rewriting if empty** will keep Views from rendering your rewrite results text, this option hides anything else you might output using field options, such as a label, prefix, or suffix text.

Finally, there is an option that works well with numeric fields, **Count the number 0 as empty**. String fields return an empty string if there isn't any information in the field. But a numeric field will return zero, which is a nonempty string. So, using this option, if a field is set to zero, then Views will act as if the field returned an empty string instead.

Okay, we've gotten through the no results behavior, so we can do our conditional value. This uses a bit of a trick. Let's use your PDF file link for title as an example case. In this version, what I want to do is link to the PDF file if it exists. But unlike the way it works now, where an empty field simply links to the home page, which when you think about it is an empty URL for the PDF file, I want to link to the node itself."

Starting at the end

"To figure out how to do this, you actually need to think backwards. Pick the value you want if the field is empty and get it ready. If this requires rewrite results, you'd do this rewriting in the field with one exception. In this case, as we aren't doing any complex rewriting, we can use the **No results text** field to generate the alternative.

For our example, we need to add the node ID field to our view, make it hidden, and rearrange the fields so that it is above the PDF file field.

At this point, if we were doing something more complex, we could set up the rewrite of the node ID to be the link URL we want in the node ID field using the **REWRITE RESULTS** option. As we don't want to specify the base URL in the rewrite, which would cause the link to always go to production or whatever base URL we specified, we'll just use a relative URL. We could use the **REWRITE RESULTS** field options to get Drupal to make the URL absolute, but for our purposes, this isn't necessary.

Alternatively, what we'll do here is actually put the same token template into the **NO RESULTS BEHAVIOR** text field in the PDF file field options. What we'll add is:

```
/node/{{ nid }}
```

Sadly, the only way to see the available replacement patterns is to open the **REWRITE RESULTS** fieldset, select the **Override the output of this field with custom text** option, look at the replacement patterns, copy the one you want, then deselect the option you picked to see the patterns, and paste the result where you want it.

So, what we have is the main field options set up to return the URL of the file via the field formatter option we selected. Then, in the **NO RESULTS BEHAVIOR** field, we added a link to the node body knowing that all the nodes can be reached using the /node/node_id pattern. This looks similar to the following:

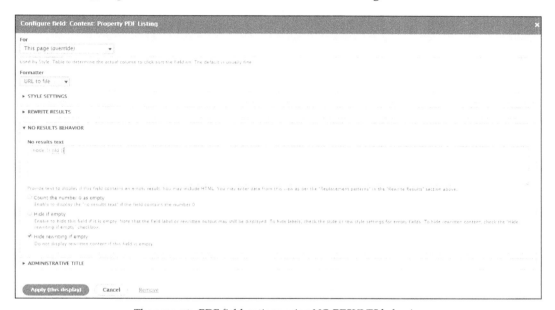

The property PDF field options using NO RESULTS behavior

So, we will end up with a view that is structured like the following:

The conditional formatting view with preview

The results are links to the PDF file if it exists; otherwise, the links go to the node.

Going beyond two levels

I've seen three levels of fall back using this technique, but it gets pretty complex. In theory, there is no limit to the number of levels. The key is working backward from each field, so the other fields are higher in the fields list and set up to be output. Then, you start with the first field, output it if it exists, and output the next highest field otherwise. This field is set up the same way; if it exists output it, use the next highest field otherwise, and so on for as many levels as you want.

While the only test you can actually do with this technique is to see whether the field is empty, I think it might be possible to use the Views Field View module to create a view using the powerful filters and contextual filters to return either an empty result if the filters aren't satisfied or a useful or useless string if they are. This result could be tested using this technique to decide whether to use the result or not.

As mentioned before in the **Override the output of this field with custom text** field section, you can put full Twig syntax into the **Override the output of this field with custom text** field. Using that undocumented "trick", you could reduce the if-then-else problem to something like the following:

```
{% if condition %}
  {# put your output for true here #}
{% elseif condition %}
  {# put your else if true output here #}
{% else %}
  {# put your default output here #}
{% endif %}
```

Other uses for field rewrites

I've also noticed something similar where a developer created a block view with conditions that test the value of fields and so on and then output a single field, **Global: text**, which contains the contents of the block. This is a way around block visibility if you can't use custom code to accomplish the special conditions, but you need more than standard Drupal block visibility criteria.

"Enough digression; did I cover everything you need to know for field rewrites?"

Lynn felt a bit overwhelmed but saw a lot of potential, so she answered, "Yes, thank you so much for the thorough explanation. I can see all sorts of field rewrite opportunities that I can incorporate into the site. I really appreciate you taking so much time to go over all this."

"No problem. You are our ideal customer, so spending time teaching you lets you do the work we'd have to assign to a developer. That frees them up for more interesting work. I'll talk to you on HipChat soon. I've got to run; I promised my wife I'd pick up our kids from school."

Summary

Views' ability to rewrite results is one of its most powerful features. Almost any output format can be created in a results rewrite. We started by showing how you can configure a richly formatted link to any content or external site. Then, we did a simple rewrite of content to make the open house display look better, followed by a more complex rewrite to add more information to the property map. Finally, we looked at how to do a conditional rewriting of a value to allow an if-then-else like logic.

In the next chapter, we'll cover the rest of the options in the center column of the view edit page. Custom headers, footers, and special messages if a set of filters (defined, exposed, or contextual) results in no results. Finally, while we looked at the Views pager a little during *Chapter 6, Add-on Modules,* when we switched to the infinite scroll module, there are various ways of dealing with a larger number of results, such as a view all link or using the powerful pager built into views to show a fixed number of results on each page and let the viewer navigate among the results.

8
Customizing Views

In this chapter, we will finish going through the configuration options in the first two columns of the Views edit screen. Most of the first column — view format, fields, filters, and sorting options — were covered in the previous chapters in detail. The second column — display settings, header, footer, no results behavior, and pager — are covered in this chapter. For many site builders, this will cover most of what they will ever use in Views.

Display settings

"Okay, Jackson, are you ready to learn more about Views?" Lynn asked Jackson as he brought a new toy filled with catnip to play with while he hung out with her as she worked. He was busy chewing on the toy. "I hope you are enjoying that catnip mouse; let's stick to toys and not find any more real mice."

"We've pretty much covered the first column of the Views edit screen: **FORMAT**, **FIELDS**, **FILTER** and **SORT**. I guess we did skip over **TITLE**, but this isn't very exciting; it changes the title for the selected display, so this would be the page title for a page or a block title for a block. It's pretty straightforward."

"Let's move on to the second column of the Views edit screen. When I select a page display, I see different settings in the top section than if I select a block display. It would appear that each display type has a different set of settings. So why not explore them all, right, Jackson?" Jackson wasn't paying attention.

"What do you say we go through the display types alphabetically?" Lynn created one of each display type in an existing view, planning on clicking on **Cancel** after she looked at each one.

Attachment

"We actually went through these settings when we did the attachment while we discussed relationships, but let's review each setting:

- **Attach to**: This determines which display or displays this attachment display should be attached to. As these are checkboxes, I can select more than one.

- **Attachment position**: This determines whether the attachment is supposed to be displayed before or after the display it is attached to.

- **Inherit contextual filters**: This determines whether this attachment should use the same contextual filter values as the display it is attached to. For this to work if selected, the same contextual filters need to be defined for the attachment and the display it is attached to.

- **Inherit exposed filters**: This determines whether this attachment should use the same exposed filter values as the display it is attached to. For this to work if selected, the same filters that are configured to be exposed need to be defined for the attachment and the display it is attached to.

- **Access**: This setting determines whether this display has any restrictions on who can see the results. Access can either be no one, or anyone can see the results, based on permission or role. Picking permission-based access allows me to pick one permission to use to determine whether the results are visible, but picking role-based gives me checkmarks, so I can select more than one role. It would appear that for most views, the default is the View published content permission."

Block

"Okay, let's look at blocks, something we use a bit more often. The settings for blocks are:

- **Block name**: This is the name or title that is displayed on the block layout page. This page can be confusing, so it is a good idea to make it clear which block this is.

- **Block category**: This is a grouping for blocks to help make the potentially long list more manageable. It is an autocomplete field, so as I type a category name, Drupal will display the options that are already set up. However, if I type in a new category name or mistype an existing name and click on **Apply**, it will be added as a new category. The default value is **Lists (Views)**.

- **Allow settings**: This setting determines whether the number of items set for the pager can be changed in the block settings options. While the screen implies that there are other settings that can be allowed, this is just the one setting for the pager.

- **Access**: This is the same as for attachment. In fact, it would appear that every display has the same access options.

Embed

- "**Access**: This setting determines whether this display has any restrictions on who can see the results. Access can either be no one, or anyone can see the results, based on permission or role. Choosing permission-based access allows me to select one permission to use to determine whether the results are visible, but picking role-based gives me checkmarks, so I can choose more than one role. It would appear that for most views, the default is the View published content permission."

Entity Reference

- "**Access**: Another display with no settings other than the access permissions."

Feed

"Good, I was beginning to think that only blocks and pages had more settings than access. Feeds have a couple of options:

- **Path**: This is the URL of the RSS feed being produced by this display. Very often, it ends in .xml as feeds are XML. Depending on whether there are contextual filters for the view, the path may have wildcards to pass them through to the view. The help text for the field says: **This view will be displayed by visiting this path on your site. It is recommended that the path be something like "path/%/%/feed" or "path/%/%/rss.xml", putting one % in the path for each contextual filter you have defined in the view.**

- **Attach to**: This determines which display(s) should show an RSS icon that is a link to the path. The setting uses checkboxes, so more than one display can be selected. The feed icon is available only to the selected displays. Unlike the attachment, the feed icon only appears after the display it is attached to. Not selecting any display to attach to will keep Views from displaying the RSS icon, but it is relatively easy to build a block to display it on the appropriate pages with more flexibility in where you want it placed.

- **Access**: This is similar to the other displays."

Page

"Well, Jackson, we've seen the settings for the page quite a few times. Let's go over them and make sure there aren't any tricks we've been missing:

- **Path**: This is the path of the view. It can have % placeholders for contextual filters, which we have already learned. I see from the field description that I can also put named route parameters, such as `%taxonomy_term`, in the path. I'm not sure I've used this before." Lynn sent Jim a message on HipChat:

    [Lynn] Hey Jim, what is a "named route parameter" in a view's path?

    [Jim] Tells Views which parameter you want rather than depending on position to use it as a default. Read this: `https://www.drupal.org/node/2186285`.

"Wow, I didn't know that paths are routes, and the parts between slashes are parameters. I guess that makes some of what I have seen for paths make sense. I don't see anything special other than trying to remember not to make my most common mistake—putting a slash at the beginning of the path. Drupal does it for me. Funnily enough, if I put the path in without a leading slash, when it is displayed it gets it added in.

- **Menu**: It looks like there are two settings here. The first makes this page display show up on a menu, much like the menu settings in a node edit form. To not have it be part of a menu, I can set it to **No menu entry**. Regular menu items would be **Normal menu entry**, and it looks like the settings are similar to what I see on a menu edit page. The other two options are **Menu tab** and **Default menu tab**. It looks like they make my menu items tabs on a page instead of making them part of a menu. From what I can see by reading `https://www.drupal.org/node/1578582`, I need at least two tabs before they display; a single tab just disappears. And a default menu tab is like a regular menu tab, but at the same time, it becomes the main page for the tabs. This should only be used if there isn't already a main page available.

- **Access**: This looks like it is just like the other displays, so there's nothing new here."

REST export

"Okay, Jackson, I know from Google that REST is the way a website talks to another. I wonder what settings there are for the REST export display:

- **Path**: The field descriptions says: **This view will be displayed by visiting this path on your site. You may use "%" in your URL to represent values that will be used for contextual filters: For example, "node/%/feed". If needed you can even specify named route parameters like taxonomy/ term/%taxonomy_term**. I don't think this makes much sense and has to be Views simply reusing the same field as displays that actually generate pages for people. Reading the section on Drupal.org, it looks like the REST path is a URL that the other website would ask to transfer and can add a format string to say how the website wants it formatted and get back not a displayable webpage but structured data, usually XML or JSON. This makes total sense, doesn't it, Jackson? It makes as much sense to you as it does to me, but I am gathering that REST export displays are used by Jim's developers and not site builders like me.

- **Access**: Again, this is similar to the other displays, except that the username and password are included in something called the header of the request. Okay, I get how this works more or less and can trust that Jim's developers know how to do headers.

Let's move on down the center column of the view edit screen, okay, Jackson?" Jackson looked up at Lynn, recognizing that she said his name but otherwise remained more interested in his toy mouse than in what Lynn had been telling him.

"It looks like the next three options, Header, Footer, and No Results Behavior all work the same way and just display the results in different locations on a page or block. They display as:

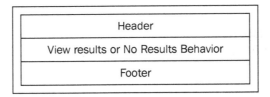

Since they all work the same way and have the same options they can display, we can do the header, and the other two are done too."

Header, Footer, and No Results Behavior

Clicking on **Add** in the **HEADER** category brought up a large list of possibilities to insert in the header. "I don't remember so many options in my old site, although I have to admit I limited myself to the **Global: Text area** option. I guess there were a half dozen options in Views 3 and now there are more than 20. And I'm not sure how to use most of them. I think I'll just make a list of them in my notebook and experiment with them if and when I ever need more than the **Global: Text area** or **Result summary** option.

"So Jackson, this also looks like an area where Drupal hasn't finished converting Views to Drupal 8. Some of the replacement tokens available in **Global: Text area** are in the old Drupal 7 format, enclosed in square brackets as in `[view:title]`. Other replacement tokens use the new Twig template format, enclosed in pairs of squiggly brackets as in `{{ arguments.field_property_neighborhood_target_id }}`. It also looks like most of the replacement patterns, if I select the **Use replacement tokens from the first row** option, don't show in the available tokens, although an earlier view experiment looks like they actually work using the tokens from the last field's rewrite results option.

When I click on **Add** in the **FOOTER** category, I get the same list of possibilities, and the same for **NO RESULTS BEHAVIOR**, so I'm guessing that they all use the same configuration code, and the only difference is where, or when in the case of **NO RESULTS BEHAVIOR**, they are displayed. **HEADER** displays before the output of the view, **FOOTER** displays after the output of the view, and **NO RESULTS BEHAVIOR** replaces the output of the view if there aren't any results to show. This is pretty straightforward, Jackson! Look at this table for more clarity:

Option	Description
Empty Node Frontpage behavior	This provides a link to the node add overview page.
Messages	This displays messages in an area.
Response status code	This alters the HTTP response status code used by this view, mostly helpful for empty results.
Result summary	This shows the result summary—for example, the items per page. It is a text area with tokens that start with @ and contain statistics about view results such as the number of records, start and end record number, and so on.
Text area	This provides markup text for the area.
Unfiltered text	This adds unrestricted custom text or markup. This is similar to the custom text field.
View area	This inserts a view inside an area. Options are a select list of the available views/displays and an option to inherit contextual filter values (such as an attachment).

Options for Header, Footer, and No Results Behavior settings Part 1

Option	Description
Rendered entity - Block	This displays a rendered Block entity in an area. Options are Block ID and View mode.
Rendered entity - Comment	This displays a rendered Comment entity in an area. Options are Comment ID and View mode.
Rendered entity - Contact message	This displays a rendered Contact message entity in an area. Options are Contact message ID and View mode.
Rendered entity - Content	This displays a rendered Content entity in an area. Options are Content ID and View mode.
Rendered entity - Custom block	This displays a rendered Custom block entity in an area. Options are Custom block ID and View mode.
Rendered entity - Custom menu link	This displays a rendered Custom menu link entity in an area. Options are Custom menu link ID and View mode.
Rendered entity - Feed	This displays a rendered Feed entity in an area. Options are Feed ID and View mode.
Rendered entity - File	This displays a rendered File entity in an area. Options are File ID and View mode.
Rendered entity - Shortcut link	This displays a rendered Shortcut link entity in an area. Options are Shortcut link ID and View mode.
Rendered entity - Subscription	This displays a rendered Subscription entity in an area. Options are Subscription ID and View mode.
Rendered entity - Taxonomy term	This displays a rendered Taxonomy term entity in an area. Options are Taxonomy ID and View mode.
Rendered entity - Tour	This displays a rendered Tour entity in an area. Options are Tour ID and View mode.
Rendered entity - User	This displays a rendered User entity in an area. Options are User ID and View mode.

Options for Header, Footer, and No Results Behavior settings Part 2

Pager

"Okay, Jackson, let's look at the last setting in the second view edit column: pager. We'll be finished soon.

Pagers allow views to display a lot of data without creating a page that could be infinitely long. Drupal defaults to showing 10 items per page and using a full pager. I know from experience with my old site and building views so far that if I set the number of items per page to 0 when I create a new view, the pager will be disabled, and the view will display everything. For my test site with a few properties, this probably is fine, but if I were on the national multiple listing service with maybe a million properties, showing all them on the same page would take forever to display and be useless to navigate.

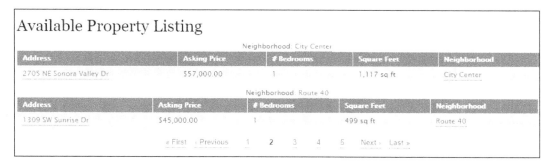

Available property listing with full pager

Replacing Drupal 7's mini pager

I also remember Jim saying that the default pager is a resource hog that will significantly slow down my site when the total possible number of items to display gets big as the pager first counts how many possible items will be displayed. I know that on our old site we have a Views Lite Pager module, but I don't see a Drupal 8 version of it." She pinged Jim again on HipChat:

[Lynn] What about Views Lite Pager for Drupal 8?

[Jim] Not needed, the mini pager for Views got changed to a lite pager early in the inclusion of Views into core. If you're interested, check out https://www.drupal.org/node/1901290.

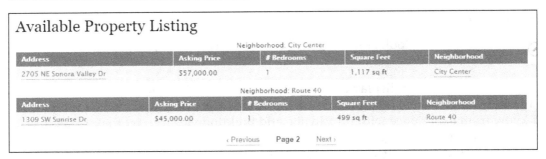

Available property listing with mini pager

"See, Jackson, Views lets you select how you want to deal with paging, even after you create the view. If I click on the pager type, I can see a list of the options, as it is here:

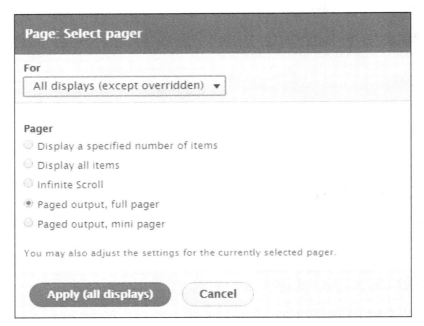

Pager options selection, including the contributed module pager, Infinite Scroll

So, I see the full pager, the mini pager, an option to display all the items or just a fixed number of items, and finally the Infinite Scroll pager from the contributed module. So, contributed modules can add additional pager options.

When I select **Display a specified number of items**, I see the configuration option for how many to display and an offset, which is labeled as the number of items to skip and defaults to zero. This would let me display five items, starting at the second item in the list as defined by my sort criteria. I've seen this in the most recent content blocks but without the offset. I guess there are use cases for being able to skip something in the list, maybe because the most recent content is displayed as a featured item with more detail, and the next five most recent content items are just titles with links in a block in a sidebar.

Pager options

For pagers, it looks like they have pretty much the same options, except that the mini-pager doesn't have options to change the labels for the first and last (because it doesn't allow this, which is why it works faster) or for how many page selection options to display (again, because it doesn't precalculate the options). And it looks like there are options to let users decide whether the pager is configurable and if so, how they can control it. Look at this table:"

Option	Description
Items per page	This is the number of items to display per page. Enter 0 for no limit.
Offset (number of items to skip)	For example, if you set this to 3, the first three items will not be displayed.
Pager ID	Unless you're experiencing problems with pagers related to this view, you should leave this at 0. If you are using multiple pagers on one page, you may need to set this number to a higher value to conflict with the ?page= array. Large values will add a lot of commas to your URLs, so avoid it if possible.
Number of pages	This is the total number of pages. Leave it empty to show all the pages.
PAGER LINK LABELS	
First page link text*	" First
Previous page link text	‹ Previous
Next page link text	Next ›
Last page link text*	Last »
EXPOSED OPTIONS	
Allow user to control selected display options for this view	

Option	Description
Allow user to display all items	
Allow user to control the number of items displayed in this view	
Number of pager links visible*	This specifies the number of links to pages to display in the pager.

Pager options list (* - are for full pager only)

Adding No Results and Footer to Available Property Listings

"Okay, Jackson, let's apply what we've learned to the *Available Property Listing* views we've already built. So, we'll start with a no results message." Clicking on **Add** next to **NO RESULTS BEHAVIOR**, Lynn selected **Text Area Global**, her go-to display for headers, footers, and no results, and kept the default **All Displays**. Clicking on **Apply (all displays)**, she entered her no results message, adding a sad face image she had uploaded earlier, and the message looked like this:

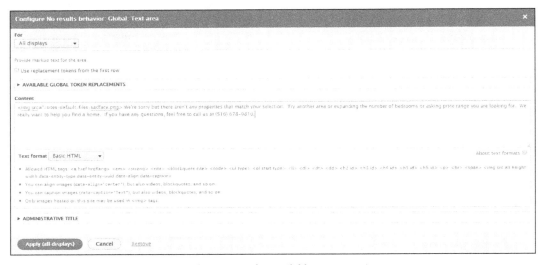

No results message for available property views

Clicking on **Apply (all displays)**, Lynn said "This was straightforward, so let's add the standard disclaimer to these same views."

Clicking on **Add** next to **FOOTER**, Lynn selected **Text Area Global**, kept the default **All Displays**, and clicked on **Apply (all displays)**; she then entered the disclaimer that her attorney insisted she display with property listings. The footer message setting looked similar to this:

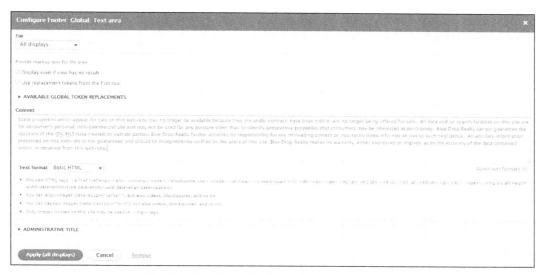

The disclaimer footer for the available property views

As Lynn was beginning to finish up, Jackson had gotten tired of his toy and started playing with the wires in the back of Lynn's monitor. Suddenly, her monitor went black, "Oh no, Jackson! You unplugged my monitor, and I hadn't saved my view yet" Lynn scolded him. She stood up, moved Jackson to one side and looked at the tangle of wires behind the monitor. One was loose and fell off the monitor. She plugged it back in and the monitor came back to life. Before sitting down, she picked Jackson up and put him on her lap. "Fortunately for you, sir, nothing was lost. Let me save this view, and we'll go join the family. I do appreciate you being here so I could talk through all these Views options. You were a big help." She gave him a nice stomach rub and then clicked on **Save** to save the view she was working on and logged out, and they were off to another room. Lynn made a mental note that she needed to take some time to organize the cables behind her monitor and screw the cables in tight so that Jackson couldn't knock them loose again.

Summary

This chapter completes describing all the standard features of Views, those contained in columns one and two of the view edit screen. So far, we have covered View Types, displays, field options, filter and sorting options, display settings, headers, footers, no results behavior, and pagers. We also covered relationships and contextual filters from the third, advanced column.

In the next chapter, we'll finish covering view options with the rest of the advanced column. In the next chapter, we'll look at an option to put the exposed filter in a block for more flexibility in their placement on the page. We'll also work through the fields under **OTHER**, Views' catchall group of obscure and relatively seldom-used options. However, they do offer some capabilities that are extremely powerful when you need them. Many site builders never need any of these settings, but knowing they are there and what they do can help you as you move to advanced displays using views.

Advanced View Settings

9

We're getting near the end of all the Views options: the third column, labeled **Advanced**. Unless you changed the default setting in the Views settings page, this column looks empty, as the **Advanced** column is a fieldset that defaults to closed. Open it up, and there are quite a few options. Contextual filters and relationships were covered in *Chapter 4*, *Contextual Filters*, and *Chapter 5*, *Relationships*. This chapter will cover the rest of the advanced fieldset. Some settings are relatively straightforward, such as putting exposed filters in a separate block and the machine name, administrative comment, and CSS class. Others, such as aggregation, caching, and the query settings, are definitely advanced settings that most users will likely never need but can offer powerful enhancements to those edge case requirements.

Becoming advanced

The next day, Lynn picked up the phone and called Jim. "Hi, Jim", she said when he answered.

"Hi Lynn, what can I do for you?"

Revisiting Header/Footer options

Lynn set the stage by saying, "I think I'm getting pretty comfortable with Drupal 8, especially with the Views module. I went over the middle column of the Views edit screen and understand most of the settings, although some of the options for header/footer don't seem to be very useful. I presume that's just because I'm not an expert."

Jim responded, "I'd say you've become an expert in the last few weeks. To be honest, I wonder about some of these options myself. I presume that they are a result of the way almost everything has become an entity in Drupal 8, and once they exposed the use cases that made sense, the rest just came along for a ride. That being said, I'm sure someone will eventually find a use for them."

"One thing I wish you could do in Headers and Footers is have entities with fields and then use the same kind of rewriting we have in fields to build the header or footer. This would be really powerful. Moving on to finish my apprenticeship in using Views, I've been looking at the **Advanced** view settings column, and about half of them don't make any sense at all." Lynn asked, "Do you have time to explain them to me sometime this week?"

"Sure, shall we meet at the usual place on Thursday evening about 7:00 pm while your son is doing Kung Fu?"

"That sounds great! I really appreciate your time. I need to take you and Sally out to a nice dinner sometime this month; let me know when and where you'd like to go."

"Ok, I'll check with Sally and tell you on Thursday", was Jim's answer. They said goodbye and hung up.

On Thursday, they met at Starbucks. After getting their drinks, they sat down at a table, and Jim brought out his computer. He logged into the development server and navigated to edit a test view they were using for experimenting. "Okay, let's go over the **Advanced** options column. I see that you have your Views setting set to always show the advanced settings, and that's certainly my preference. Why don't you go down the column and tell me which settings you understand from your experimenting and learning so far?"

Lynn took a look at the third column's settings, which looked similar to the following:

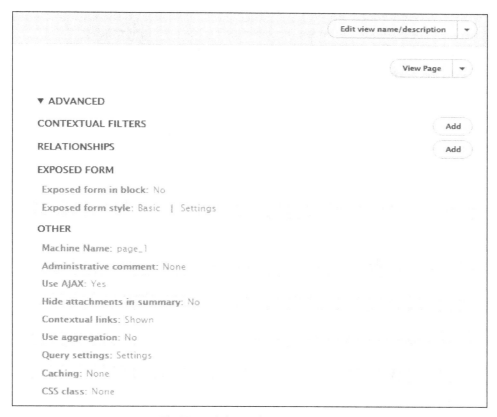

The Views Advanced settings column

Contextual filters and relationships

Lynn started, "Contextual filters and relationships we covered in detail already, so I feel comfortable with them and their settings. I sort of understand the exposed form setting, but I'm not clear on the exposed form style options. Machine name is pretty obvious, it is what views calls this display internally. I'm not sure why I'd ever change it, though. Pretty much the rest of the column doesn't make sense, except the last setting, which I figured out sets a custom CSS class, or classes, on the outermost div of the view."

Advanced options

"Okay, that's about what I would have expected, so let's just go through the options that you don't understand." Jim then continued in his teaching mode.

Exposed form in block

"Let's start by looking at **Exposed form in block**," he said as he clicked on the **No** link to show the options:

Selecting Exposed form in block

"**Exposed form in block** is a setting to let you take your exposed filter inputs and put them in a block instead of at the top of the view results. Some page layouts would be clearer if you could separate the exposed filters, which is why you'd use this option. You'll notice that it only appears for page or feed displays. Frankly, I can't think of how you'd use the option in a feed because it is a way to expose your data to another website so that they won't be looking at the rendered page; I presume it is just a bug that no one cares about enough to fix.

If you select the **Exposed form in block** option, you need to remember to add the block to the views page using the **Block layout** settings page (**Structure | Block layout**). Otherwise, your exposed filters will just "disappear." You also want to make sure the block visibility of this block is set to only display on the page that the view is on because the exposed filters really only make sense on this one page.

One point about using exposed forms in blocks is that you need to enable the **Use AJAX** option for exposed forms in blocks to work. This also explains why you can't expose the forms for a block display. As we'll talk about in a minute, AJAX requires that the main display have a URL for AJAX to work, and blocks don't have their own URL when they are on a page, so there'd be no way for the exposed form to send its results back to the view.

You mentioned the **Exposed form style** setting; it is pretty esoteric. The **Basic** setting works pretty much like you'd expect, by allowing the exposed filters to work and using the defaults you set for the exposed filters if they are empty. The **Input required** setting overrides the default setting for the filters if they are all empty and won't render the view at all. So, if you set **Input required** on your main property listing and a visitor didn't use any of the filters, there would be no listings, but as soon as any one of the filters has input from this visitor, the other filters can use the defaults, and you'll see the results. This is handy if you have a set of filters that could generate a very large result, which would take a long time to render.

The settings for the two options are almost the same, and let you change the labels of the buttons that might appear. Let's look at the **Basic** settings:

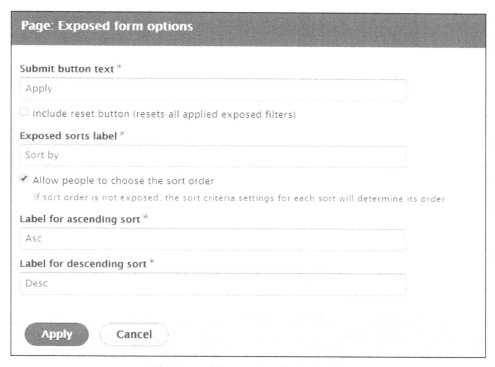

The Exposed form settings for basic style

You've got the **Submit button text** field, which defaults to **Apply**, so you can also select an option to add a reset button, and if you do, you can select its button text. Next, you have the option to expose the sort order, which duplicates settings on each sort field, but if you had a complex sort and wanted to expose all of them at once, this setting might be easier. If selected, you can change the labels for the ascending and descending buttons."

"Moving on to the **Input required** option, you'll notice almost the same settings," Jim said as he changed to the settings which looked similar to the following:

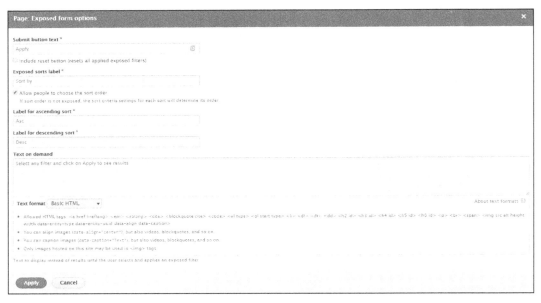

The Exposed form settings for input required style

"The only setting that is unique to the **Input required** option is what text to display instead of the view results until the user makes a selection. This is an HTML field, so you can get pretty fancy with the formatting if you want. About the only thing missing might be token support, so you could have this text make reference to something about the view. I'm not sure I can think of a use case, but that is one thing I noticed.

Using AJAX to update pages

Moving down, the advanced setting is **Use AJAX**. Let's take a look at how to turn it on:

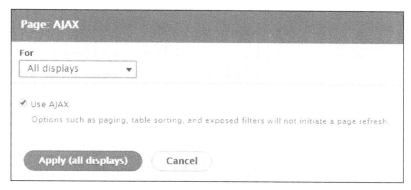

Enabling AJAX in a view

I've already mentioned that you need to use this option if you want to use the **Exposed form in block** option. AJAX is a powerful part of Drupal, so let's talk about it for about two minutes. Not only is it required for the **Exposed form in block** option, but it also changes how Views renders other things. If you look at the description on the option setting, it says **Options such as paging, table sorting, and exposed filters will not initiate a page refresh**. So, selecting this option will change how the pager and table sorts work. Instead of redrawing the entire page, which can take some time if your theme has lots of blocks on every page, Views will take the results from the view and swap it out with the next set of results from the view. As a visitor, all you see is the text magically changing from one set of results to a different set.

This magic is a result of AJAX, which stands for **Asynchronous JavaScript and XML**; it uses JavaScript, a programming language built into every browser, running in the browser to ask for data from the website, which is converted to HTML by the JavaScript code and inserted into the page when the website sends it back. To make it easier for JavaScript to work with this data, instead of HTML, the website returns XML, which is a more general version of HTML that lets developers represent structured data. Of course, if you have JavaScript turned off, which some companies do to increase security, then Drupal will fall back to redrawing the page each time something changes, and your exposed filters won't be displayed or work.

You've been using AJAX for quite a few years. The first really important use of AJAX was Gmail, all the way back in 2004, joined by Google Maps in 2005. Actually, AJAX was invented by Microsoft way back in 1998; instead of using JavaScript, they had an ActiveX control that updated content on the default Internet Explorer MSN page. However, it's Gmail that really got AJAX started on a track to become a real industry standard, and a lot of the major sites use it or some variant of it.

I'd say you should select this option when you can unless you notice problems resulting from using it, which can happen, especially if you have a page with more than one view, as it will make your pages appear to load faster and won't cause reloads, which can be distracting.

Hiding attachments and enabling contextual links

The next option, **Hide attachments in summary**, is used for those views that have an attached display, such as your property listing that shows the open houses as an attachment that caused you preview headaches. In this view, if you had the exposed filters set to display some summary, such as the total number of available properties, instead of all the results when exposed filters didn't have a valid result (either being present or an input that didn't pass the validation criteria), then you probably don't want to display any open houses either. So, setting this option will hide the open house attachment until the view actually displays results, and then it will show the corresponding open houses.

The **Contextual links** option just lets you hide the edit view contextual links for a given view or display. Let's say that you give other users permission to edit some views but don't want to make it too easy to change a particular view; in this case, you can set this option to **Hidden**, and the option to edit the view won't be displayed. If this were a block display, the option to configure the block would still show up as a contextual link, but the option to edit the view wouldn't.

Changing the SQL queries generated by views

"The next two options, **Use aggregation** and **Query settings**, are pretty complex and change the very heart of Views—the SQL queries it generates. As I've said before, Views is a report writer for Drupal. As Drupal allows structured data (thanks to fields), it stores its data in a database, and not all content management systems do this, you can take this data and use SQL queries to create the many different kinds of displays you've been building. And for most Views users, they will never need to know any SQL; Views will do it for you.

Of course, professional programmers scoff at the SQL queries generated by Views. It has to make a lot of assumptions, so it doesn't always generate the most efficient SQL queries required for the display. However, this can usually be offset by Drupal's caching, even by an external cache such as Varnish, because most Drupal data doesn't change by the second, or for many sites, by the day.

Query settings

Let's start with the **Query settings** option, as it is a bit simpler to explain and set the stage for using aggregation." Jim clicked on the **Settings** link and showed Lynn the following page:

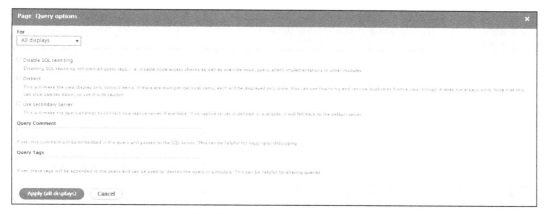

The Views Query Settings options

"The first option, **Disable SQL rewriting**, effectively turns off changes from external modules for this view. The way Drupal operates in general is that one contributed module, or the core itself, can generate some content. Then, other contributed modules can alter this content using hooks and more in Drupal 8 PHP plugins. This all happens at the programming level, which is why this is unlikely to be an option that you will ever use. However, it is possible that some other module does something to alter your output, so as the very last resort, you could change this setting and it would disable the hooks inside Views so that you get exactly what you generate. If this is the answer, then you can start looking at the contributed modules you have installed and see whether any of them change the SQL query. I usually do this by performing a search of the contributed module folder.

The next option, **Distinct**, is actually an option you might need. Its description actually says a lot about its use case: **This will make the view display only distinct items. If there are multiple identical items, each will be displayed only once. You can use this to try and remove duplicates from a view, though it does not always work. Note that this can slow queries down, so use it with caution**. Let's say you want to create a view of the properties that have open houses but not display the start time or the end time. If you create a simple view of the Open House content type, you'd get a line for each open house, so it would have duplicated properties in the list. In some rare cases, using the distinct option would return just one result per value. As it turns out, in this case, this wouldn't work. To understand why, let's use the generated SQL to see what's going on.

A simple view of open house titles would generate SQL that looks similar to the following:

```
SELECT node_field_data.title AS node_field_data_title, node_field_
data.nid AS nid
FROM
{node_field_data} node_field_data
WHERE (( (node_field_data.status = '1') AND (node_field_data.type IN
('open_house')) ))
ORDER BY node_field_data_title DESC
LIMIT 10 OFFSET 0
```

Adding the distinct option changes the resulting SQL query to look similar to the following:

```
SELECT DISTINCT node_field_data.title AS node_field_data_title, node_
field_data.nid AS nid
FROM
{node_field_data} node_field_data
WHERE (( (node_field_data.status = '1') AND (node_field_data.type IN
('open_house')) ))
ORDER BY node_field_data_title DESC
LIMIT 10 OFFSET 0
```

So far, it looks like it should work. However, the way the SQL DISTINCT keyword works is that it needs everything in this query to be the same to be distinct. But as Views included the node ID (or nid) field, which is unique to each result, no two results have the same combination of title and nid, even though the first three have the same title. So, the distinct option will not work for us. I get the feeling from the look on your face that I just went way too deep into the insides of how Views works, but my point was to show you that this option doesn't always work; in fact, it only works in rare cases. There's another option that we'll talk about in a minute, aggregation, which can often solve the problem. However, using distinct is always worth a shot.

Reading from a secondary database server

The **Use Secondary Server** option is used on some large sites with a lot of data but wouldn't do anything for you. On larger sites, there is often more than one database server, usually operating in a master/slave configuration. The master gets all the writes to the database, and the slave is kept synchronized by MySQL. Then, if something goes wrong and the master crashes, which fortunately doesn't happen very often, the slave can be promoted to master and a new slave built.

If your site gets a lot of traffic and you have views that can't be cached for whatever reason—for instance, they display data that is being updated continuously; think of a website showing the current status of every train in New York Metro—then you might exceed the capacity of the database server to handle the load. As most of the load usually generates the displays, one option would be to let the content editors and our real-time feed use the master database to store updates and let site visitors use one or more of the slave, or secondary, database servers to make their read requests. It is relatively easy to add more than one slave to a single master, so as traffic scales, you could have more than one slave server to handle the load. This is one of the many techniques used by the Grammy website, which goes from a few thousand visitors a day to about ten million visitors an hour during the broadcast.

Most sites don't have the secondary database defined to Drupal, so even if they use a master/slave configuration for redundancy, Drupal can't use the slave. It isn't hard to set up in the Drupal configuration file; it's just not frequently done. If it is and you set the **Use Secondary Server** option, then Drupal will start reading from this slave server. The good news is that if you don't have a slave server defined to Drupal, then this option basically does nothing, so setting it by accident won't change anything.

Developer options

The last two options, **Query Comment** and **Query Tags**, are used by developers. They are used to identify queries during development. The difference is how. Query comment simply puts a comment into the query, which is handy if you are stuck debugging a query to the level that you resort to the MySQL logs to find out what is going on. You can search for the comment. The **Query Tags** option is often used if you have a custom module that needs to alter a SQL query and needs to know which one. You might have a couple of views defined that look almost exactly the same, except that one is changed by your module. You'd add a query tag to this view, and then the module can test for the presence of the tag to decide that the query it is trying to alter is the one it needs to alter.

Using aggregation

The **Use aggregation** option is the other way you can remove duplicates and much more. If you click on **No** and select the **Aggregate** option, then many of the fields in both the fields to output and the sort and filter area, even contextual filters, will now show a new option link, **Aggregation settings**. So, a complex view such as your available property listing view would have a dozen or more aggregation settings options available, such as this relatively simple view:

Fields showing the Aggregation setting link

Fortunately, the default is basically do nothing, so that is good. When you click on one of the **Aggregation settings** links, you will see a bunch of options that look similar to the following:

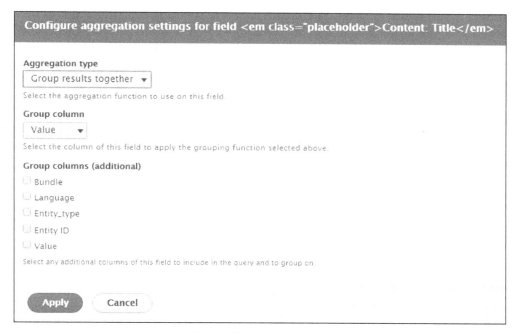

Aggregation settings options

Aggregation type

The **Aggregation type** option determines how the aggregation will operate. The default option **Group results together** is what you would use to only output a single result per value—in the open house case we were discussing earlier, one result per property. However, aggregation can do manipulations also. The other **Aggregation type** options are: **Count**, **Count DISTINCT**, **Sum**, **Average**, **Minimum**, **Maximum**, and **Standard deviation**. The difference between **Count** and **Count DISTINCT** is best shown using our example. **Count** would show the five open houses, but **Count DISTINCT** would show two, which is the number of unique results for the field. Most of the options allow various statistical results to be displayed instead of the value of a field.

Grouping

The other two settings, **Group column** and **Group column (additional)**, let you specify the aggregate based on something other than a field's value. Drupal stores a whole lot more with each field value, such as what content type this value is attached to, what language, and so on. Remember that you can actually do a view of one content type, not select by this type, and display a field from another content type. Why so, I'm not too sure, but it can be done in Views. Also, some content types share fields, such as a common e-mail field, so a view on this field could be set up to display all the e-mail addresses stored on the site, then use aggregation to remove any duplicates from the list, and use the resulting list for e-mail blasts. Or you could select the count option and group by entity type and get a count of how many e-mail addresses you have in each type. But this would only work if you use shared fields, which many Drupal sites don't do for maintainability.

While aggregation settings can be set on each field shown, the resulting query would be extremely complex and likely not result in much by way of results. Other than perhaps using the same field more than once in the display section and using aggregation settings to get statistical results by selecting different options to display, I wouldn't recommend even trying to use more than one per view. Plan on spending some time experimenting to get the right combination of settings and rewriting output to make it work the way you want.

Making Views go fast

The last setting, **Caching**, is actually very important for Drupal performance. I'm surprised to see this view has caching disabled. If you remember way back when you started on this learning journey, one of the advanced Views general settings is to disable caching on a global basis. The description for this option says that it will have a serious performance impact on your site, which is really true. Views is a SQL query builder that can generate complex and time-consuming database queries. You don't want to execute them any more than you have to, especially if your data doesn't change in real time, which is true for most websites.

Caching types

Assuming you want caching, you need to decide what kind. One option is **Time based**, which is the kind of caching most used by Drupal 7 and before. This option basically says "wait for some period of time", an option that appears if you select the option when rerunning the query if you have already run it before. After this period of time, the results stored in the cache are invalidated, and the query is rerun.

If your data changes and something doesn't manually invalidate the cache results, you might not see the new values until the time period elapses. So, if you set the time period to 3 hours, then it could be 3 hours after you change a property from available to under contract if you use time-based caching.

In Drupal 8, the caching system has been significantly reengineered. Drupal 8 actually puts various tags on every part of your Drupal site. These tags can show what is dependent on what and how. So, if you have a view that uses user information, then Drupal 8 knows that it needs to have a different cached copy of the view for each logged-in user. Similarly, a view that displays a node that changes will know that the node has changed via its tags and it has to rerun the query to regenerate the results. It is amazingly powerful, and I'm just starting to even realize that it is part of Drupal 8, so I suspect as we all learn more about this caching option, we'll discover that even though Drupal 8 is hugely bigger than Drupal 7, it can actually serve similar pages faster. This is especially true for external caches, such as Varnish, which many sites use to make the site capable of handling a lot more traffic for a given-sized server. This allows some lower-priced hosting options to work well, even shared hosting, which was pretty much not an option for most Drupal 7 sites with any kind of traffic. So, unless you have problems and one of our developers has looked into the cause, I'd say leave the **Caching** setting at its default, **Tag based**.

So, do you think you understand the rest of the **Advanced** settings column and when you might use them?"

Lynn replied, "Thanks for explaining all that. You're right, I can see where understanding the SQL queries generated by Views and how to adapt it could become a full-time job and specialty. But I think I understand enough to be able to build out my site and make changes. By the way, did Sally ever pick a date and place for dinner?"

Dinner plans

Jim had an embarrassed look on his face as he said, "Thanks for reminding me, I had forgotten to tell you. How about this Sunday at Le Petit Maison? That's Sally's favorite restaurant in town, and her parents can take the kids for the night so that we can make an evening out of it."

Lynn shrugged and said, "Perfect, I'll make a reservation for 6 pm, and we'll meet you there. I think I've gotten enough of the site ready that it's time to make the move to Drupal 8. Let's start the process of migrating all the properties from the old site and doing the design and theming to make it look modern and fresh. Is there anything I can do to help make the theming go easier?"

"Actually, there might be. Why don't we get together next Wednesday morning at our offices? Our designer can have some comps for the design we've been talking about for you to review and approve. And if you have some extra time, I can go over how Views and theming interact. By then, the developers should have been able to do the migration from your current Drupal 6 site to Drupal 8. If you can keep track of any edits you make between now and when we go live, it will help. While we can rerun the migration just before the site goes live, it helps to have an idea of what we should double-check. Also, if we don't have to rerun the migration, it saves time and your money."

"That's really fast, Jim. I'm always impressed with how you can get big projects done so quickly. Wednesday morning works for me, and we'll see you Sunday night for a nice dinner. And no talking business during dinner, okay?"

"Sounds good to me! It's nice to get away from work now and then. See you on Sunday."

Summary

In this chapter, we completed our exploration of the Views edit screen by looking at the advanced settings. Contextual filters and relationships were covered in depth in the previous chapters. Many of the remaining settings are straightforward, and in some respects, the **Advanced** settings column is a sort of miscellaneous settings collection. However, a few are very powerful, such as **Use AJAX**, which will change the way your website renders content that is spread across several subpages. Others change the SQL queries being generated to combine the results, which is important if there is a lot of data to display, and this detail isn't relevant to site visitors.

In the next chapter, we'll finish our dive into Views by learning how to theme the output of the views you generate so that they look exactly like you or your designer had in mind. We'll start with some relatively easy adjustments to the CSS classes generated by views. Once we've exhausted our options from the user interface, we'll move to adjusting the Twig templates used to generate the HTML code. Between the two, it is unlikely that there is a view that can't be styled exactly as you want.

10
Theming Views

In this final chapter of the book, we'll look at theming the Views output and changing the look of what you generated using Views. For a lot of websites, just being able to add and change some CSS classes and the occasional HTML tag used is sufficient to get the look you want. However, if you have to go further, you likely will need to change the templates used to render the SQL results into HTML.

Time to theme

Sunday night's dinner ended up being very pleasant for Jim, Lynn, and their spouses. The restaurant was packed, but their reservation got them seated quickly. With the help of their spouses, Jim and Lynn were able to keep the discussion of Lynn's new site to a short status update on the design. The rest of the evening was spent in small talk, mostly about what the children were doing.

The following Wednesday morning, Lynn walked into Jim's offices for the appointment to review the designs with the designer that worked for Jim. They sat in the conference room. Jim said, "I see you brought your own coffee, so it would be redundant to offer you some."

"Thanks, but Starbucks was on my way walking over here, so I stopped," replied Lynn.

Designing mock-ups for the new site

"Then, I guess we're ready to get started. Sam has a great concept that captures your goal to have a modern, clean redesign of the website. We will go from the busy, three-column look of the current Drupal 6 site to an edge-to-edge fluid design that is fully responsive. With the growing number of visitors coming to the site from mobile phones, this is really important." Jim showed Lynn the design for the front page and for an inner page.

After looking at the mockup drawings for a few minutes, Lynn said "Wow, this is really nice. I'd like to change the color of the menu to a dark blue to better fit into our color scheme, but other than that, I like the concept. Jim, let's move ahead with this design. And can your developers move the data from the old site, especially the properties? There are a couple of hundred active listings, and I'd hate to have to input them over and over again. We can definitely leave the old listings behind on the old site if that makes it less work." With a big smile on his face, Jim answered "Sure, we can move your data; it's called migrating. It will take a developer a couple of days to set up the migrate module in Drupal 8, and then when you are ready to make the new site live, we can rerun the migration to make sure it has the latest data. Also, we can move as much or as little of your existing data as you'd like. It's all in getting the migration set up; then, running it is easy."

Turning to the designer, he said, "Sam, as always, you did a great job finding a contributed theme to adapt rather than developing a theme from scratch. Clients such as Lynn really appreciate the results. Tell the development team to make the changes we discussed as a subtheme; that way, we can update the contributed theme if updates come out, which I would expect this early in the Drupal 8 release cycle."

After Sam left the room, Jim said "I want to repeat that I'm really impressed with how much you've learned about the ins and outs of Views. You are at par with any of our developers. If you want to switch careers, we are hiring."

"Thanks, but I have enough to keep me busy running Blue Drop Realty and helping build our new site. I like the new design, the site is about ready to have your team theme it, and your development team will migrate the properties from the old site to the new one. What can I do to help?"

"Well, as you did all the Views on the site, it is possible that the frontend developers will want to tweak some HTML code to make the design even better as they adapt the theme. If you want, I can have you make these changes; that way, you'll know what has changed when you go back to modify or add new views. Does that sound reasonable?"

"Sure. As you know, I don't know any CSS to speak of, but I recognize most HTML code I see. How hard is what you're asking?"

"Actually, a lot of what might be needed can be done through the Views UI. Occasionally, we need to do something that can't be done with CSS; then, we work with the theme templates, which is programming that doesn't look like programming, and I'm confident you can do what's needed. And, of course, we're here to answer any questions you have. If you have some time this morning, I can walk you through theming options for Views."

"The design review went a lot faster than I would have expected, so sure, let's do it now," was Lynn's eager response.

"Ok, let's refill our coffee cups, and I'll grab my computer."

Changing generated HTML and CSS from the Views UI

Once again, Jim went into teaching mode using a copy of the development site on his computer to demonstrate what he was describing.

Structure of a View's output

Taking out a pad of paper, Jim drew a box and labeled it **View**. Then, he drew two smaller boxes inside and labeled them **Row**. Finally, inside each of the smaller boxes, he drew even smaller boxes and labeled them **Field**. The resulting picture looked similar to the following:

The Views structure diagram

"If you think of the results of a view as being the view in its entirety, which might include headers or footers, then you have a number of rows, and each of these rows has a number of fields. Each of these levels can have CSS classes attached to them to make generating customized theming easier. Alternatively, a lot of our developers just use the many divs and their associated classes, even though they might not be as semantic sounding as "front-page-row" or "featured-title". However, let's say you want to add a CSS class to each level. You can do this using just the Views UI.

The entire View CSS settings

We actually looked at the View-level CSS setting last week when we went through the **Advanced** settings options. One of the last options is **CSS class**. So, if we change this option to, say, **front-page-featured-properties**, then save the view and go to the front page, where the featured properties block is displayed, and then when we view the source and search for **front-page-featured-properties**, we'll see that the HTML code looks similar to the following:

```
<!-- THEME DEBUG -->
<!-- THEME HOOK: 'views_view' -->
<!-- BEGIN OUTPUT from 'core/themes/classy/templates/views/views-view.
html.twig' -->
<div class="front-page-featured-properties contextual-region view
view-featured-properties view-id-featured_properties view-display-id-
block_1 js-view-dom-id-2227695de747adc95968bd49f4b2a9a439639157b44206d
847202010f78909a7">
```

Theme debugging

The theme debug HTML comments are generated by the built-in theme core theme helper that was created for Drupal 8. It will be vital later when we talk about templates, but for now, just know that it is there on your development site; we usually turn it off when the site moves to production. I'll tell you how to turn Twig debugging on and off a little later. What it is telling us here is that the class we defined is added in front of all the normal Views generated classes on the outermost div generated by Views.

Also, if you make a change such as this and don't see the class you added, try clearing the Drupal caches a couple of times. Both Views and the theme system are heavily cached as they can slow a site down if they weren't. Sometimes, it takes that second cache clearing to finally get what you want to show.

It was clear where to look for the setting to change the CSS class for the whole view; at least it is clear if you have the **Advanced** settings fieldset opened. The setting for the rows is actually hidden a bit. I'm not sure I would have predicted you'd find the setting row CSS classes in the Display Format settings modal, but this is where it is located. Many kinds of formats, such as the slideshow contributed module, might add even more configuration options for the CSS, and all formats offer a couple of settings.

Row CSS

The first, **Row class**, is just like the **CSS class** setting at the view level. It lets you add one or more CSS classes to be the outermost div for each row. And this operates in the same way. One interesting feature of this setting is that you can use the same tokens that you would have used while doing a field rewrite but at the row level; so, in theory, you could have a field that contains the CSS class to apply to the row and use its value in the HTML code for this row. That's pretty slick in my mind.

The second is a checkbox that is labeled **Add views row classes**. Its description states: **Add the default row classes like views-row-1 to the output. You can use this to quickly reduce the amount of markup the view provides by default, at the cost of making it more difficult to apply CSS**. It is enabled by default, but if you clear the checkbox, then Views won't output its usual CSS classes. So, let's look at the simplest configuration setting options for an unformatted list in a block:

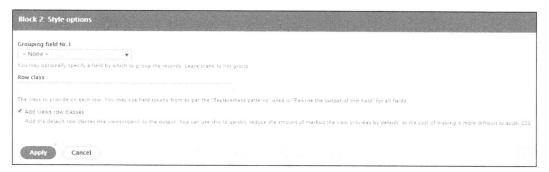

The CSS settings for an unformatted list in a block

See, it's pretty simple. So, we've covered the entire view and each row, and the last set of options is for individual fields.

Field HTML and CSS

In the case of fields, the settings are actually part of the field options, so when you click on the field name in the view and open the **STYLE SETTINGS** fieldset, the options look similar to the following:

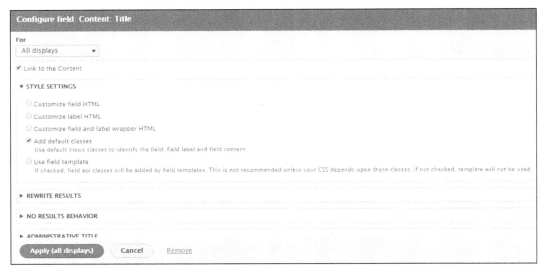

The style settings for a field, where each option displays additional settings

Let's select the first option, **Customize field HTML**. When you select the option, additional settings appear, which look similar to the following:

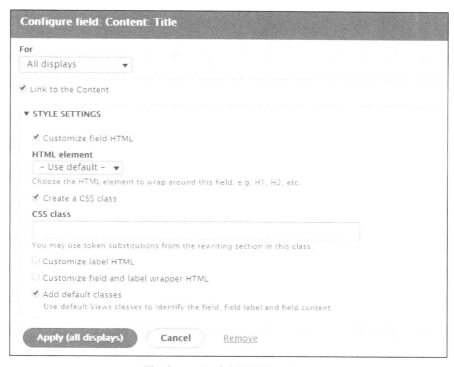

The Customize field HTML settings

The first option lets you change what tag to wrap this particular field in. Typically, it is a div, but this can change depending on the type of format selected. However, in this very comprehensive drop-down, you can make it almost anything, including some very esoteric HTML tags that I had to look up to even know that they were legal. Take a look at this list of options:

- Use default -, - None -, DIV, SPAN, H1, H2, H3, H4, H5, H6, P, HEADER, FOOTER, ARTICLE, SECTION, ASIDE, DETAILS, BLOCKQUOTE, FIGURE, ADDRESS, CODE, PRE, VAR, SAMP, KBD, STRONG, EM, DEL, INS, Q, S

The other option is selecting our familiar **Create a CSS class** option and then a field to give the CSS class you want to use for this field.

Not only can we set the wrapper and class for the field, but we can also use different settings for the field label if it is output. Also, there is a third setting for a wrapper that surrounds both the label and field values. Between these three sets of settings, I can't imagine not being able to get HTML code that will work. And, as many of the tags are HTML5, this means that we can have fields that automatically display differently on mobile devices and might even add functionality.

Note that the next option in **STYLE SETTINGS** is **Add default classes**. This is just like the row setting, if you clear the checkmark, Views won't output its usual CSS classes.

The last option is **Use field template**. This setting defaults to disabled, not checked. If you read the description, it says **If checked, field api classes will be added by field templates. This is not recommended unless your CSS depends upon these classes. If not checked, template will not be used**. What the setting actually does is add a second template while rendering the output of a field. So, if you don't select it, then the `views_view_field.html.twig` template is used. If you do select it, then the `field.html.twig` template is used inside the `views_view_field.html.twig` template.

That setting actually leads us to the next part of theming Views output, which is using theme templates to change the HTML being output. Let's get a coffee refill, and then we'll tackle templates."

Lynn agreed, "All these settings and what they do have my head swimming, so a break sounds perfect."

When the HTML code needs to change

"Okay, we've looked at the changes you can make to the CSS classes, and for fields, the HTML tag wrapping the field output. Another place that you already know we can put CSS if we have to is the field rewrites. In fact, I have seen you being very creative in using field rewrites to combine fields in ways I would never have thought of.

However, let's say you need to do something more than you can with a field rewrite or that you don't want to have this kind of logic in your view; your option then becomes modifying the theme template to change the HTML code at this level.

Of course, there are some modifications that require more logic, perhaps coupled with database manipulations that go beyond what can be done with templates. These should be done in a custom module rather than in a template. The rule of thumb is that you can put conditionals and loops into templates and can do a reasonable amount of string and math manipulations in templates, but once you get to functions or database queries, you need to be in a custom module.

A quick review of the Drupal 8 theming changes

Prior to Drupal 8, theme templates were combinations of HTML and PHP programming called **PHPTemplate**. As you can put any kind of PHP programming in these templates, I've seen some absolutely terrible things done. An obvious one is putting database queries in the template. But perhaps the worst one I saw was a Drupal 6 site that did IP address-based location sensing in the page template, then switched the Drupal language setting, and started rebuilding the page in a new language. The page template is just about the last step in the process, so doing that wasted all the effort when it switched languages.

Drupal 8 switched theme templates to Twig, a different way to abstract what it used to be in HTML. One positive point of switching to Twig is that it is really hard to put these really bad practices into your template; they simply won't work.

Twig also is more secure. A lot of Drupal security issues are a result of not sanitizing user inputs when displaying them. This lets a bad user possibly exploit a site. I'd say 99% of the time, the developer simply forgets about the security implications and to use the built-in functions that Drupal has to clean up text. Twig now automatically sanitizes all output to get to the raw input you need to explicitly tell it that you know what you're doing with this string.

Drupal 7's PHPTemplate version of views-view.tpl.php

Let's look at the outermost template used by Views in both the older PHPTemplate versions:

```
<div class="<?php print $classes; ?>">
  <?php print render($title_prefix); ?>
  <?php if ($title): ?>
    <?php print $title; ?>
  <?php endif; ?>
  <?php print render($title_suffix); ?>
  <?php if ($header): ?>
    <div class="view-header">
      <?php print $header; ?>
    </div>
  <?php endif; ?>

  <?php if ($exposed): ?>
    <div class="view-filters">
```

```php
      <?php print $exposed; ?>
    </div>
<?php endif; ?>

  <?php if ($attachment_before): ?>
    <div class="attachment attachment-before">
      <?php print $attachment_before; ?>
    </div>
<?php endif; ?>

  <?php if ($rows): ?>
    <div class="view-content">
      <?php print $rows; ?>
    </div>
<?php elseif ($empty): ?>
    <div class="view-empty">
      <?php print $empty; ?>
    </div>
<?php endif; ?>

  <?php if ($pager): ?>
    <?php print $pager; ?>
<?php endif; ?>

  <?php if ($attachment_after): ?>
    <div class="attachment attachment-after">
      <?php print $attachment_after; ?>
    </div>
<?php endif; ?>

  <?php if ($more): ?>
    <?php print $more; ?>
<?php endif; ?>

  <?php if ($footer): ?>
    <div class="view-footer">
      <?php print $footer; ?>
    </div>
<?php endif; ?>

  <?php if ($feed_icon): ?>
    <div class="feed-icon">
      <?php print $feed_icon; ?>
    </div>
<?php endif; ?>

</div><?php /* class view */ ?>
```

Drupal 8's Twig version of views-view.tpl.php

Here's this same template in the new Twig version:

```
{%
  set classes = [
    'view',
    'view-' ~ id|clean_class,
    'view-id-' ~ id,
    'view-display-id-' ~ display_id,
    dom_id ? 'js-view-dom-id-' ~ dom_id,
  ]
%}
<div{{ attributes.addClass(classes) }}>
  {{ title_prefix }}
  {% if title %}
    {{ title }}
  {% endif %}
  {{ title_suffix }}
  {% if header %}
    <div class="view-header">
      {{ header }}
    </div>
  {% endif %}
  {% if exposed %}
    <div class="view-filters">
      {{ exposed }}
    </div>
  {% endif %}
  {% if attachment_before %}
    <div class="attachment attachment-before">
      {{ attachment_before }}
    </div>
  {% endif %}

  {% if rows %}
    <div class="view-content">
      {{ rows }}
    </div>
  {% elseif empty %}
    <div class="view-empty">
      {{ empty }}
    </div>
  {% endif %}
```

```
{% if pager %}
  {{ pager }}
{% endif %}
{% if attachment_after %}
  <div class="attachment attachment-after">
    {{ attachment_after }}
  </div>
{% endif %}
{% if more %}
  {{ more }}
{% endif %}
{% if footer %}
  <div class="view-footer">
    {{ footer }}
  </div>
{% endif %}
{% if feed_icons %}
  <div class="feed-icons">
    {{ feed_icons }}
  </div>
{% endif %}
</div>
```

You'll see that they are pretty much the same, except for the syntax used. In PHPTemplate, you see lots of `<?php print` plus something, an occasional `if` conditional, and a few calls to the `render()` function, which takes the Drupal render arrays used to store output until it is converted into HTML and does this conversion.

Twig variables

One huge difference is that Twig is really smart about variables. So, in PHPTemplate, you might have seen something similar to the following:

```
<?php print $node->field_open_meeting['und'][0]['value'] ?>
```

In Twig, it would just be as follows:

```
{{ node.field_open_meeting.value }}
```

Our developers used to spend a lot of time figuring out which variable array indexes to use to get the value of a field, usually by putting in debugging print statements. And sadly, they can change, especially if your site is multilingual, generating errors later that you didn't see before simply because the language code has now become significant, where when we were setting up the theming for the site, there wasn't any multilingual content to test with.

Now, in Twig, the logic of finding a value is built into Twig. All you need to do is specify the variable you want. A lot of Drupal's information is stored inside arrays and, increasingly, objects as well—worse, as my example shows, arrays within objects that might be inside arrays! It used to drive us crazy. Now, with Twig, we just specify the component with a period, and Twig figures out whether it is an object or array automatically. Twig also takes care of getting the right language automatically. Switching to Twig is really a huge win for our frontend developers. Also, this is a win for sites we inherit because it makes it really hard for a developer to not use the Drupal way and stick code into a theme template that doesn't belong there but should have been in a module.

Enabling theme/Twig debugging

One last new feature in Drupal 8, which has been backported into Drupal 7 as of 7.33, is the addition of theme debug. In Drupal 8, in our `/sites/default/service.yml` file around Line 38, are some Twig configurations that we can change for our development environment to enable debugging. The comments do a good job of explaining them, as follows:

```
twig.config:
  # Twig debugging:
  #
  # When debugging is enabled:
  # - The markup of each Twig template is surrounded by HTML comments that
  #   contain theming information, such as template file name suggestions.
  # - Note that this debugging markup will cause automated tests that directly
  #   check rendered HTML to fail. When running automated tests, 'debug'
  #   should be set to FALSE.
  # - The dump() function can be used in Twig templates to output information
  #   about template variables.
  # - Twig templates are automatically recompiled whenever the source code
  #   changes (see auto_reload below).
  #
  # For more information about debugging Twig templates, see
  # https://www.drupal.org/node/1906392.
  #
  # Not recommended in production environments
  # @default false
```

```
      debug: true
      # Twig auto-reload:
      #
      # Automatically recompile Twig templates whenever the source code
changes.
      # If you don't provide a value for auto_reload, it will be
determined
      # based on the value of debug.
      #
      # Not recommended in production environments
      # @default null
      auto_reload: null
      # Twig cache:
      #
      # By default, Twig templates will be compiled and stored in the
filesystem
      # to increase performance. Disabling the Twig cache will recompile
the
      # templates from source each time they are used. In most cases the
      # auto_reload setting above should be enabled rather than
disabling the
      # Twig cache.
      #
      # Not recommended in production environments
      # @default true
      cache: false
```

By turning theme debug on by setting debug to true, Drupal will put HTML comments in every page that shows which template naming options are available and which is currently being used. This is tremendously useful and eliminates the need for the old **Theme Devel** module, which did something similar through JavaScript, which, in turn, almost always "broke" the formatting of the page. We'd enable it, find the template information we need, and then have to disable it to see what we were doing. Now, we can simply view the source.

Views templates

Now that we've taken a side track into how theming has changed, let's get back to how we might want to use the templates for Views to change the output.

If you look back at the diagram we drew of how the Views output is structured, the templates work pretty much the same way. There is an outer template for the view, and inside this template are blocks of output that were rendered by other, subsidiary templates. We might view the templates as being nested similar to this:

The Views template nesting for the Selectable Property Listing display

```
html.html.twig
  page.html.twig
    block.html.twig
      views-view.html.twig
        form.html.twig
          views-exposed-form.html.twig
            form-element.html.twig
              form-element-label.html.twig
              input.html.twig
            form-element.html.twig
              form-element-label.html.twig
              input.html.twig
            container.html.twig
              input.html.twig
        views-view-table.html.twig
          views-view-fields.html.twig
            views-view-field.html.twig
            views-view-field.html.twig
            views-view-field.html.twig
        pager.html.twig
        container.html.twig
          views-view.html.twig
```

As you can see, Drupal 8 uses a lot of templates. This makes it very flexible to change the output of a view or anything else created by Drupal 8.

In reality, the rendering happens from the bottom up. The most nested template is rendered and returned as a variable containing the resulting markup. The next most nested template does its thing, using the variable that contains the bottom-level template's markup to output this part of the output, which is returned as a variable to the next higher-level template. This continues until Drupal reaches the `html.html.twig` template, which is the highest-level template in Drupal, and this template returns the fully formed HTML page that is returned by Drupal for this page. It took me a while to really starting thinking about how the nested templates worked, so don't be surprised if you spend some time wondering where something is actually getting rendered. Fortunately, the output of theme debug really helps with this.

It is interesting looking at the nesting of templates that the header and footer don't have templates associated with them. I have a feeling that this was an oversight, but it does mean that we're forced to put more into these text areas than we would have preferred because we can't put our HTML, classes, and so on into a template.

What I've just shown you is using the default templates for each level. However, suppose we wanted to change the output for just one view. We can do this as Drupal has a very flexible template naming system that will try a series of template-suggested names until it finds one that exists, ending at the template shown in this example.

Template suggestions

Views doesn't offer a lot of template suggestions, but to show how the concept works, let's look at the template options for the page that the selectable view is located on. Drupal follows this pattern:

```
page--[front|internal/path].html.twig
```

So, the possible options for our selectable view are:

```
page--available-property-listing-selectable.html.twig
page.html.twig
```

So, if we look at the outermost view template, the naming options for a view with the machine name machine_name are:

```
views-view--machine_name--page.html.twig
views-view--page.html.twig
views-view--machine_name.html.twig
views-view.html.twig
```

Every template usually has theme suggestion options. A lot of Drupal core template names are shown at https://www.drupal.org/node/2354645. But Views hasn't been added to this list yet.

If we don't see an option that works, we can also use a custom module that implements hook_theme_suggestions_HOOK to add additional template name suggestion options or hook_theme_suggestions_HOOK_alter to change the existing template name suggestion options.

This pretty much covers template and template suggestions. I can see by your eyes that I lost you about halfway through this, but I wanted you to see what is available. Someday, you'll find one of our developers saying something about overriding a template, and hopefully, you'll remember enough of this to have an idea of what they are talking about. Sorry I went so deep, but I am excited by how all this works in Drupal 8."

"No problem, Jim," was Lynn's reply. "I understood some of what you were showing me, and if nothing else, it gives me an idea of how flexible the deep-down theming in Drupal 8 can be. I hate to say this, but I really do have to run. I have a meeting with a client in about 15 minutes. Thanks for taking the time to go through this with me."

"You're welcome and good luck with the client. Let me know when you are ready to have us take the site live."

Going live and accolades

A week after Lynn's meeting with Jim and the rest of his team, the site was ready to go live. Jim's team had migrated a copy of the development site, including the code, database, and user files, onto the production servers. On that momentous day, Jim contacted the domain registrar and changed the IP addresses for the bluedroprealty.com domain. A couple of hours later, visitors to the site were surprised and impressed.

Later that year, at the annual realtor's conference for the state of Missouri, the bluedroprealty.com website won an award for the best locally produced website of the year. Lynn was excited when she got the news and shared it with Jim.

"Jim, you aren't going to believe this!"

"Well, hello Lynn. Long time no talk. I presume all is well with your new site?"

"Not only is it running better than it ever did in Drupal 6, but it also just won the state realtors association award for the best website of the year!"

"An award justly deserved, even if I do say so myself. You did a great job of putting a lot of great content together with amazing displays to make it easy for people to find what they need. Congratulations to you."

"It wouldn't have been possible without the power of Views and your help. Thank you so much for all you've done during this conversion. Please pass my thanks on to the rest of the team there."

"No problem, and don't stay a stranger. We can chat without having Views questions to discuss, you know. And my offer to hire you as a developer still stands."

"I promise we'll get together next week. I've been so busy with inquiries from the new site that I really haven't had a lot of time."

Summary

This chapter covered theming the output of Views from simple CSS additions that can be managed directly from the user interface, to using Twig templates, to completely changing the HTML code generated by views. Twig is a big change in Drupal 8 theming and worth learning.

That's the end of this book on mastering Views. I hope you have enjoyed following Lynn's adventures as she learned all about how to get the most out of Views to create flexible and powerful displays of the collections of content. Remember that this book just scratches the surface of what is possible with Views. Your imagination and the willingness to experiment with what Views does are the only limits. I'd like to leave you with a picture of the "real" Jackson. He doesn't belong to Lynn but to one of my co-workers at WebNY, Meredith Case:

The "real" Jackson

Content Types for a Sample Site

If you want to follow along with the example site, the following sections describe the content types defined on the site used throughout the book.

Property

The title field is renamed Title-Address 1.

Label	Machine name	Field type
Property Address 2	`field_property_address_2`	Text (plain)
Property Asking Price	`field_property_asking_ price`	Number (decimal)
Property City	`field_property_city`	Text (plain)
Property County	`field_property_county`	Entity reference (County)
Property Description	`body`	Text (formatted, long, with summary)
Property Featured	`field_property_featured`	Boolean
Property Featured Image	`field_property_featured_ image`	Image
Property Geolocation	`field_property_ geolocation`	Geolocation
Property Image Gallery	`field_property_image_ gallery`	Image
Property Listed Date	`field_property_listed_ date`	Date

Label	Machine name	Field type
Property Neighborhood	`field_property_neighborhood`	Entity reference (Neighborhood)
Property Number Bathrooms	`field_property_number_bathrooms`	List (text)
Property Number Bedrooms	`field_property_number_bedrooms`	Number (integer)
Property Owners	`field_property_owners`	Entity reference (Property Owner)
Property PDF Listing	`field_property_pdf_listing`	File
Property Realtors	`field_property_realtors`	Entity reference (Realtor)
Property Square Footage	`field_property_square_footage`	Number (integer)
Property State	`field_property_state`	Text (plain)
Property Status	`field_property_status`	List (text)
Property Zip	`field_property_zip`	Text (plain)

Property Owner

The title field is renamed Full Name or Company.

Label	Machine name	Field type
Owner Address 1	`field_owner_address_1`	Text (plain)
Owner Address 2	`field_owner_address_2`	Text (plain)
Owner City	`field_owner_city`	Text (plain)
Owner Company	`field_owner_company`	Text (plain)
Owner Email	`field_owner_email`	E-mail
Owner First Name	`field_owner_first_name`	Text (plain)
Owner Last Name	`field_owner_last_name`	Text (plain)
Owner Phone	`field_owner_phone`	Telephone number
Owner State	`field_owner_state`	Text (plain)
Owner Zip	`field_owner_zip`	Text (plain)

Realtor

The title field is renamed Full Name or Company.

Label	Machine name	Field type
Realtor Address 1	field_realtor_address_1	Text (plain)
Realtor Address 2	field_realtor_address_2	Text (plain)
Realtor City	field_realtor_city	Text (plain)
Realtor Company	field_realtor_company	Text (plain)
Realtor Email	field_realtor_email	E-mail
Realtor First Name	field_realtor_first_name	Text (plain)
Realtor Last Name	field_realtor_last_name	Text (plain)
Realtor Phone	field_realtor_phone	Telephone number
Realtor State	field_realtor_state	Text (plain)
Realtor Zip	field_realtor_zip	Text (plain)

Open House

The title field is not renamed.

Label	Machine name	Field type
Notes	body	Text (formatted, long, with summary)
Open House End	field_open_house_end	Date
Open House Property Reference	field_open_house_property_refere	Entity reference (Property)
Open House Start	field_open_house_start	Date

County Taxonomy

This has no custom fields.

Neighborhood Taxonomy

This has no custom fields.

Index